Sober On A Drunk Planet:
The Challenge

- A 31-Day Guided Sobriety Journal
With Prompts And Daily Reflections For Living Sober

(Alcohol Recovery Journal)

By Sean Alexander

This Challenge is dedicated to Patrick.

Without those searching questions and a safe space to share my inner thoughts and feelings, I would still be drunk or probably dead.

TABLE OF CONTENTS

INTRODUCTION

A journey of a thousand miles starts with a single step
— Lao Tzu.

How many times have you said to yourself, after waking up with yet another horrendous hangover, that next week will be the week that you finally make those positive changes you've been promising yourself for years?

When that hangover is so bad, you can't even summon the energy to change the TV channel. You just about have enough energy to make it to the front door for your pizza delivery. All while you mindlessly roll into work the next day and start the same negative feedback loop of drink > regret > repeat – this is your chance to stop that cycle and begin to see the superhuman powers you can achieve when you stop drinking alcohol (and "superhuman" might even be an understatement!).

Whether you hit rock bottom like I did, losing everything to alcohol and drugs, or you just don't like the poisonous effects of alcohol on your mind, body and soul - then this 31-day challenge is a great starting point to transform every area of your life.

It will help you break free from that negative feedback loop that has held you captive to achieving your hopes and dreams. Or maybe it's held you back from even starting to think outside of the weekly "session" and it's time to start levelling up with bigger goals, dreams and a life you can be truly proud of.

The fact you've picked up this challenge is powerful evidence you want to stop drinking, but you need a little help. That's okay. Quitting alcohol can be one of the biggest challenges you ever overcome, but you *can* do it. Millions of others in worse positions than you have successfully given up alcohol and, if appropriate to your situation, other drugs as well, to lead exciting and fulfilling lives – so there is no reason why you can't join them.

We live in a society where alcohol is constantly used as a social lubricant. We pull out a bottle to celebrate birthdays, Christmases, christenings, and holidays. We turn to alcohol to support us through the tough times when a relationship ends, we've had a hard time at work, we've fallen out with a friend, or we're simply feeling tired and depressed. We have a drink to pick us up. We have a drink to relieve boredom. We have a drink to give us courage and confidence. We have a drink to chase away the hangover from the night before.

Any excuse, right?

It's no wonder so many of us believe that alcohol is the cure for just about anything. We live on a drunk planet.

Yet when we take a step back, it's not quite the wonder juice we might think it is. Chances are, there's at least one Alcoholics Anonymous or SMART Recovery group within easy reach of where you live. (We will provide the links later on so you can see for yourself.) You may be surprised at just how many groups are nearby – ask yourself, why is that?

Why do we think it's OK for someone to drink right up until the point they drink so much they do something embarrassing? Why is the alcohol-free industry booming? Why is alcohol the only drug we have to justify to strangers about NOT drinking?

Everybody had an opinion about my cocaine use, but nobody thought my chaotic behaviour under the influence of alcohol was anything to worry about?!

The answer can be boiled down to one fact: when you stop drinking alcohol, life opens up in ways you never thought possible.

They're discovering that the night before isn't worth the hangover the morning after (or half a week if you are over thirty years old!).

They're finding that they enjoy remembering all the fun they had on an evening out instead of having to contact their friends in a panic to fill in the blanks left by an alcoholic blackout.

They're realising that when you lose your alcoholic crutch and stand tall on your own two feet, you get to explore life's full potential – and it's beautiful.

How do I know all this? Because I lived it. I was genuinely sick and tired of feeling sick and tired by the time alcohol and drugs had destroyed my life. Sobriety for me was not just about giving up alcohol and other drugs; it was about doing the work to find out why I became addicted to drink and drugs in the first place. Going to rehab, going to individual therapy, journalling, group therapy in the form of Alcoholics Anonymous meetings, re-training as a counsellor, strength and conditioning coach and writing a book series on alcohol and its harmful impact on our lives all had a part to play.

Whatever part of the rock bottom to social drinker scale you might be on, there is always work to do around why you drink the way you do – is it trauma? Is it anxiety triggered by being bullied as a child? Is it a lack of confidence and self-esteem? Is it a mix of the above? The level of work you have to do will vary on the severity of your relationship with alcohol. I can guarantee that journalling will help you become more self-aware of those challenges.

This challenge isn't about me; it's about helping you make healthier choices, become more self-aware and encourage you to take positive actions that will help keep you sober. I strongly recommend that you read my other books in the Sober On A Drunk Planet series, *Giving Up Alcohol* and *3 Sober Steps*, as they will provide invaluable resources to refer back to as you complete this challenge and beyond.

This challenge is a perfect complement, giving you practical support as you break free of the control alcohol has over you. This journal is designed to be like a counsellor being by your side each morning and night, there for you as you learn more about yourself, discover your triggers, and develop healthier habits that will stay with you long after the alcohol's gone.

The journalling prompts will challenge your thinking because the way you think about alcohol is flawed. This challenge will give you the time, space and questions needed to break free from alcohol's hold on you so you can be armed with the self-awareness required to create a new sober life. A life that is exciting, fulfilling and better than any life you had when alcohol was robbing you of time, energy and money.

The Challenge

If you want to win the three major prizes of more time, energy and money, then completing this 31-day challenge will give you the boost you need to make sobriety a lifestyle you will never want to escape from.

The prizes go far beyond more time, energy and money (which are pretty epic anyway!), and the fun starts when you start seeing all the benefits for yourself.

Here is a list of some of the prizes you could win from completing this challenge:

- No hangovers – If you drank like I did, dry mouth, splitting headache, and vomit were a regular post-binge occurrence. Plus, the only cure for hangovers is sobriety (anything else suggesting otherwise is fake news).
- Becoming FIT. Alcohol robs you of consistency, and being hangover-free allows you to be consistent with your health and fitness. You will grow muscles in places you didn't even know existed!
- The ability to look ten years younger because your body is detoxing all the poison that alcohol and other drugs have been ruining your system with! (Nobody gets bored of the compliments of how well they look when they get sober).
- Improved mental health. Alcohol is a depressant, and giving it up is one of the best things you can do for your mental health. You will think clearer, faster and smarter when you are NOT hungover and depressed.
- New and exciting friendships centred on self-growth and sobriety (not based on how good your hangover is).
- A new career you love or an ability to turn up in your current job and show everyone who is the real BOSS now that you have all that energy and clarity from being sober (rather than sitting in a job you hate and getting drunk to tolerate it all).

- Money – the opportunity cost of alcohol is EXPENSIVE. Sobriety gives you all the time, energy and opportunities you need to get rich (Not just financially but spiritually, emotionally and physically).
- Time – you will be SHOCKED at how much time you have wasted on alcohol and its control. Sobriety will give you more time to do the things you have always spoken about doing but were too hungover to actually do.
- Improved sex life – no floppy dick and dry vagina to ruin your alcohol-fuelled nights out. Sobriety allows you to stay hard and moist (yes, I cringed at writing that word, but you get the point!).

These are just a few of the millions of benefits you get from staying sober – which is why nobody has ever regretted getting sober.

Becoming Sober On A Drunk Planet is one of the bravest things you can do on a planet obsessed with it all. You will also benefit from radical clarity once you are unshackled from alcohol's control. You might even find that after 31 days, you have your own "sober awakening" and become one of the millions of people who think – "why did I ever drink in the first place when sobriety feels this great?".

The challenge is to complete this guided sobriety journal with prompts and daily reflections for living sober with all your energy for 31 days. Where your attention goes, your energy flows and this should be your primary focus for the next 31 days (because the benefits of staying sober are LIFE CHANGING!).

You will get out what you put into completing this challenge and remember, "If it doesn't challenge you, it doesn't change you". This journal has been designed as a challenge to make you think and act differently and help you stay sober for the long term.

Start to think what all those benefits could mean for you – no hangovers, more time, more energy, clarity of thought, better relationships, improved sex life, a massive improvement to your career, more money and much more!

What's Different About This Challenge?

Let's be honest: there are plenty of other alcohol-free challenges you could have picked up. I want to say thank you for choosing this one. I've worked hard to make sure that it's not like any other challenge out there. It's designed to fit into your life in a way that makes staying sober insightful and fun and makes the journalling part of the challenge easy to complete.

Keep it by your bed for the next 31 days to complete each section when you wake up and go to sleep. The routine of having it by your bed should remind you that it needs to be completed at the same time each day, when you wake up and just before you go to bed. But it will be worth setting daily reminders on your phone, Alexa or other devices as an extra nudge.

As you work through the challenge, you'll pick up more information about staying sober in a way that makes it simple. I've made sure not to overcomplicate things so you can put into practice everything you learn and make changes to your routines in a way that works for you.

The exercises in this journal are built around the method of getting sober outlined in my previous book, "*3 Sober Steps*".

As part of this challenge and journalling practice, you will:

1. **Build self-awareness** (the foundation for living the life you want)

2. **Take positive action** (knowledge is only potential power: Knowledge + positive action = power to change)

3. **Build a healthy intuition you can repeat on autopilot** (repeat healthy habits on autopilot so you benefit from the sober compound effect)

This helps you break the destructive patterns caused by alcohol and drugs, such as going for a drink > doing something stupid > feeling hungover > feeling shame and remorse for getting drunk > repeat.

This challenge, with its journalling prompts and guides, is born from my experience of studying and using positive psychology, practising gratitude, and working on emotional regulation as an essential ingredient to long-term sobriety. Not only that, I've also included lessons I've learned through my personal experience of overcoming addiction but also my professional experience as a counsellor and personal trainer.

The goal of this challenge, and the rest of the Sober On A Drunk Planet books and resources, is to help you stay sober so you can break free from alcohol's control and experience the life-changing benefits that sobriety has to offer.

We REALLY want to support you all the way because we know firsthand how shit the cycle of being hungover and depressed can be. We want to help you change the narrative and help you reach your full potential – that starts with getting and staying sober.

Why 31 Days?

They say it takes 21 days to form a new habit. In reality, it's a little more nuanced than that, and it'll vary from individual to individual. By the time I went to rehab, I was fully addicted to alcohol and drugs, so it wasn't as easy as just forming a new habit, but a 28-day stay was enough time for me to break that cycle and start with a fresh perspective.

31 days covers the longest months, and the journal is designed to encourage you to stay sober beyond that (because why wouldn't you want to feel amazing 100% of the time!).

Wherever you might be on the scale of alcohol addiction, this journal will help boost your self-awareness and ability to take positive action in your sobriety journey.

Journalling was a massive part of my recovery once I had left rehab, but it was coupled with individual therapy, group therapy and emotional regulation work. I loved journalling's therapeutic nature so much that I decided to write a book series!

If you struggle to complete this journal over 31 days and find a few days impossible, this challenge will show you that you might need more support, and that's perfectly ok. Many prompts along the way will give you the information you need to get more help.

For most people, this journal will get you through 31 days of no alcohol because you aren't addicted to it, and you are still able to make conscious choices around alcohol (addiction takes away that freedom).

If you enjoy the challenge this journal helps you complete, you can always start another 31 days after you finish – the result will be even more sobriety, self-awareness and more positive actions taking you to where you want to be in life.

A Word Of Warning

Some days will be more challenging than others, and you will probably find you'll want to turn to drink to cope with withdrawal. Whether it's a physical withdrawal symptom noted below or an emotional withdrawal, e.g. hitting the "big red fuck it" button because life feels stressful.

Pushing through that irritability and restlessness is where the growth lies. I am telling you this now: it gets easier every time you push past it, and once you've done it once, the second time becomes a bit easier and so on.

And here's where we need to get serious for a moment. Really serious. The truth is that if you don't break free of alcohol, you risk doing serious harm to yourself. You may find yourself experiencing some nasty side effects when you first remove alcohol from your life. You may find yourself shaking, sweating, or even hallucinating when you stop drinking. These are all physical symptoms of alcohol dependence – and they're all highly dangerous.

You may also suffer other physical side effects such as:

- Sweating.

- Hand tremors (shakes).

- Insomnia.

- Irritability.

- Anxiety and depression.

- Appetite loss.

- Headaches.

- Vomiting.

- Nausea.

- Fast pulse (above 100 beats per minute).

- Restlessness.

- Irritability.

- Disorientation.

- Breathing problems.

(Source: Drinkaware)

While these symptoms may also have other underlying causes, it's essential to be aware of what might happen when you eliminate alcohol from your life. Even more importantly, if you're a regular drinker – and I cannot stress this enough – you should consult a medical professional before suddenly stopping.

When you're an alcoholic, your body becomes physically addicted to alcohol. It's one of the most dangerous drugs there is, and even more so because it's totally legal. While you might think you're doing the right thing by completely cutting it out without any preparation, in fact, you could be putting yourself at risk of alcohol withdrawal syndrome. Symptoms include seizures and sudden death.

If you are a regular drinker, speak to your doctor, as they can help with any physical withdrawal you might have (this challenge can't!).

And a final warning about one of the nasty side effects of sobriety, which luckily only impacts a small minority — you might be so energised by sobriety that you take up CrossFit!

You have been warned.

The Method: 3 Sober Steps

"Insanity is doing the same thing over and over again and expecting different results." — *Rita Mae Brown.*

Right now, you're probably stuck in a never-ending cycle of drinking > regretting > repeating. If you can replace those three steps with the three principles I'm about to take you through, you'll be able to live a much healthier, happier life. A life that is free from the control that alcohol has had over you all this time.

1. Self-awareness

If you're going to stay sober for the long haul, you need to understand exactly why you drink the way you drink, i.e.

the fact you have never been part of that "one and done club" (which I still don't believe exists!). It all starts with self-awareness. Connect with your emotions and recognise that our thoughts create our emotions, ultimately leading us to take action, which is how we shape our reality. It all stems from our thoughts, and we have the power to change those thoughts at any time (yes, we really do).

Have you ever been hurt by someone and decided to get shit-faced in response? Have you had a stressful week at work and decided to drink all Friday night to forget about it all? Have you ever felt anger and sent a text straight away without thinking it through? These emotions are created by our thoughts, e.g., that person dumped me, so there must be something wrong with me, and because of that thought, I feel hurt, sad, and angry. The action that comes from those emotions can be hitting the "big red fuck it" button – we then go out and get blind drunk to (wrongly) deal with those emotions.

Over time, the only emotional response you might recognise is getting drunk – whether happy, sad or somewhere between the two.

The good news is that we are not our thoughts; we can learn to understand and control our emotions better. We can choose to change or ignore our thoughts. We can learn to better understand how those thoughts create our feelings, and that allows us some freedom to control what actions we then make (as opposed to saying "fuck it" to everything and getting drunk....again). I know, I know. It's easier said than done. But it *is* possible, and it all starts with understanding ourselves better.

There are so many reasons why people drink: to rebel. To relieve boredom. To fit in. To drown their sorrows. And it can be a combination of factors as well. The journey towards alcohol addiction is a complex one, and there are many pitfalls along the way.

This journal will help you understand your personal motives for drinking so you can start unpicking your triggers and start consciously taking back control of your life.

2. Take positive action

Reading books about getting sober is great. It can be a first step towards a new way of life. But it can also be a way of kidding yourself you're taking action when really all you're doing is reading books! You can feel inspired by what you read all you like. Knowledge in books stays in books until you actually put the principles into practice. The only person who can save you is you – and you can't do that if you're not *doing* anything to make a change.

When I went into rehab, I was 31. Before then, I thought I had a pretty good handle on life. After all, I was financially successful with a high-flying career. It was a slap in the face to accept that nobody else could live my life for me. If I wanted to get sober, I had to do the work. I couldn't palm the unpleasant tasks off to an assistant.

The same is true for you. If you want a different result, you've got to do things differently. That's why this challenge is set up to prompt you to take positive action towards sobriety. This will have a positive knock-on effect, spreading into all other aspects of your life.

This journal is about you taking positive action towards staying sober and starting to see those benefits for yourself that so many of us keep banging on about. After all, who doesn't want more time, energy and money – it really is worth doing the work for.

3. Connect to your intuition

What negative patterns have you fallen into because of your drinking? Maybe you don't even know right now, and that's okay – as you work through this journal, you'll soon be able to identify those downward cycles that aren't serving you. So, for example, after-work drinks on a Friday might be an automatic response to needing to unwind after a tough week at work. Going out and enjoying those brief moments where alcohol represses feelings of stress and tension blinds you to the reality that you've just had five lousy days at work, and now you're condemning yourself to having a terrible weekend because you're going to feel hungover (again). The chances are you won't want to do anything a lot more fun than just sit on the sofa and feel sorry for yourself.

If you can find better ways of managing your stress at work and set healthy boundaries when it comes to those after-work drinks, you can stop this subconscious pattern of behaviour. It will allow you to become aware of what you're doing and why and instead replace it with what you wanted to do but couldn't because you were nursing a hangover. Wouldn't it be nice to get home at a reasonable time, wake up feeling fresh and filled with energy and do all those things you've been talking about over drinks but never got around to because of the hangovers?

If you ever feel frustrated between what you would like to do versus your actual reality, that is a sign your intuition could be talking to you. It could be saying, I really want you to do those exciting experiences, but the habit/addiction of alcohol use keeps you a slave to its control. You then feel sorry for yourself the next day and feel like you have let yourself down and maybe others as well.

That frustration or tension between what you want your life to look like and your reality is your intuition screaming at you. We all have that gut instinct that keeps us safe if only we listen. The problem is that alcohol drowns out the sound of that voice. The more we ignore it, the quieter it gets until we can barely hear its whispers. Before you know it, you are hungover on the sofa again in the same negative feedback loop. As you work through this challenge, you'll reconnect with this intuition guiding you where you want to be. Staying sober is the best gift you can give to that gut instinct and one of the life-changing prizes available for completing this challenge!

Sobriety isn't about always getting things right. It's about being able to deal with situations and not self-destruct with alcohol. Building self-awareness around our emotions and actions, which this journal will help you do, allows us to make healthier choices. Sobriety allows you to become consistent. When you become consistent in what you want to do, things get very exciting quickly.

How To Win

This Challenge has been designed to help you take the first steps toward your sobriety and complete the challenge of becoming Sober On A Drunk Planet in 31 days. It will educate you in short, easily digestible snippets so you can learn more about yourself, why you drink, and understand what you might be experiencing.

It will help you become more self-aware through daily self-reflection and honest observation and give you practical tools to stay sober so you can benefit from the countless benefits sobriety brings. These are introduced in a carefully thought-out order, so you're not overwhelmed. You can quickly incorporate them into your routine and make permanent shifts in your thinking and behaviour.

I've combined my personal and professional experiences and positive psychology to give you the best chances of staying sober.

While this journal is designed to be a standalone, you can also use it as a companion to *Sober On A Drunk Planet: Giving Up Alcohol,* which contains a wealth of information about all the benefits of giving up alcohol. In addition, you should read *3 Sober Steps* for an in-depth look at those three processes I mentioned earlier: self-awareness, positive action, and intuition, as well as further advice on how you can safely and comfortably break free of the hold alcohol has on you. The more you learn about your relationship with alcohol, the easier it becomes to choose to stop drinking alcohol.

While this journal is designed to be completed in 31 days, there is no reason why you can't come back and redo it again and again if you need to. You will always learn something new about yourself at different times, and this challenge will help deepen that self-awareness each time.

Life is a journey, not a destination. Even when you're fully sober, you should always be working on becoming as self-aware as possible about your thoughts, feelings, and behaviours. These will ultimately determine how successful you are in life – and I mean real success, the kind that leaves you feeling fulfilled and like you've found your purpose, not just how much money you have in the bank.

I cannot emphasise enough how important it is to develop self-awareness. When you don't know who you are and what you want, you become a sheep. You follow the herd to the bar every Friday night after work because you're blind to the alternatives. You stay in your comfort zone because it's what you've always known, and you kid yourself that it's safe there because the thought of doing anything else is scary – even if your soul is crying out for something different! You never get anything done you actually want to do because you have no idea what that would even look like, and you don't have the courage to follow your heart.

Self-awareness, positive action and developing a healthy intuition are the keys to true, lasting happiness. Being sober is the foundation for that happiness.

In addition, we have given you even more life-changing resources that will go a long way to helping you win this challenge. From our Sober On A Drunk Planet books, podcasts, YouTube videos, weekly emails and our fantastic community – we really want to give you access to everything to help you win this challenge and become Sober On A Drunk Planet.

Just 31 days of sobriety can be the key to unlocking a wealth of life-changing benefits. I can't tell you where this journey will take you, but I can promise you it'll be somewhere more fabulous than being a slave to alcohol.

Understanding The Journal Prompts

As I mentioned at the start, this journal differs from other sobriety journals. I've designed it to be a challenge because being sober for 31 days on a planet obsessed with it all is challenging. It's ultimately a guided sobriety journal based on my own and wider sober community experiences, which has incorporated evidence-based practices to make it a genuinely valuable, helpful tool. None of the exercises should take long, so you can easily incorporate them into your day without feeling like a chore. Hopefully, you'll find it fascinating to see what comes up as you start to explore the inner workings of your mind and unravel the complexities of your relationship with alcohol – I know I did.

Every day, you'll be given an inspirational quote and daily reflection to develop your understanding of the process and get you thinking about what's really driving you. These will be delivered in bite-sized chunks that are easy to digest, and you will be given space to write out any thoughts. If you have more to write than the space in this journal, keep an extra writing pad with you just in case you need to keep journalling thoughts down. You should keep writing until you can't write anymore – that's where the therapy is!

Below is an explanation of each of the prompts in the journal so you can understand why you are doing these and, ultimately, what the benefit of doing so is creating for you. With these prompts and the tools we are helping you develop, repetition is crucial to its success, so keep going with them until the end.

Day Journal

Today I feel...

You'll start by filling out your day journal, beginning with the prompt *Today I feel...*

We start with your feelings to get a baseline for your emotions before you get stuck into the day. The idea behind this is to build an understanding of yourself, see how your thoughts create emotions, what those emotions look and feel like and how they can affect your behaviour throughout the day.

You'll close out this exercise in the evening by asking yourself the same question and reflecting on why you think your emotions have shifted over the course of the day or if they've stayed the same, why that might be.

When you instigate this daily practice of examining your emotions, you seek to become more emotionally mature, where you can bridge a space between thinking, feeling and acting. Staying sober is a perfect example of emotional regulation when you find yourself being able to say *no* to the "fuck it" button and go to bed early/read a book/cook something/do whatever appeals to you instead of drinking alcohol because that's what you've always done. This will help keep you in the positive feedback loop, which feeds the positive compound effect in every area of your life.

It's important to understand that you need to be in charge of your emotions to make healthier choices. The practice of emotional regulation will help you create space in your thoughts so you can pause before rushing in to act on an emotion. This journaling process will allow you to find the space and time to make better choices until they become automatic. You'll be able to resist the pull of volatile emotions such as anger, sadness, and happiness.

If you're not used to consciously observing your emotions, you may find that you're so disconnected from them that you can't even identify how you're feeling at any moment. Don't worry. I've got you covered. I've included the Emotions Wheel in the Appendix. This simple graphic will help you pinpoint the primary emotion you're currently experiencing and then drill down into the specifics of your feelings. If at first you can only give a basic description of how you're feeling in that moment, that's okay. The very act of trying will gradually open you up to your emotions, and you'll soon become better at knowing exactly what you're experiencing.

I am grateful for...

Once you've taken a moment to reflect on your feelings, you'll be given a prompt to consider what you're grateful for today.

I am grateful for:

1.

2.

3.

You've probably heard about practising gratitude if you've done some research into becoming and staying sober. It's increasingly popular as a therapeutic tool because it's one of the most powerful tools available. I found it incredibly helpful because choosing to be grateful taught me how to be happy with what I have rather than focusing on the sadness and frustration I felt when I thought about what I didn't have. This also supports the work you're doing on emotional regulation – those feelings of sadness and frustration could be triggering emotions that might cause you to drink.

Some people find gratitude easy to tap into, while others need to develop it through practice and conscious effort. Wherever you are with your gratitude journey, choosing to feel grateful every day can quickly transform negativity into more positive emotions, giving you a brighter outlook on life, one filled with hope and contentment without needing alcohol just to get through.

It can be challenging at first to get into an attitude of gratitude, especially if you've been thinking negatively your whole life. But that negative thinking is just a habit. It's just a thought. And we can change our habits and thoughts and replace them with more positive ones – like gratitude.

So, maybe you found that when you examined your feelings, you woke up in a bad mood. Perhaps you had a bad dream, someone at work annoyed you, or maybe when you got up to go to the toilet, you stubbed your toe, and it's still hurting. You wrote down *I am feeling grumpy*. But then you got into your gratitude list, and you found that you were grateful you had a warm bed to snuggle into, even if you didn't sleep well. You're grateful you went out to see a movie with a friend last night instead of going to the bar. You're grateful you don't have a throbbing headache from a hangover to add to the pain of your toe.

Immediately, you feel a little bit better. It's almost like magic. And then you're starting your day in a better mood. So you don't snap at the first colleague who comes to ask you a question. You don't stomp around the office like a bear with a sore head. You don't argue with the waiter who serves you dinner. And because you don't do any of those things, your day goes better than expected and you're not tempted to have a drink at the end of it.

Gratitude works!

Practising gratitude will also help you heal the relationship you have with yourself. As you work to get sober, you may well feel guilty for your past mistakes and feel bad about yourself because you've messed up so often. While it's important to acknowledge those mistakes and do your best to make up for them as part of your recovery, you must also learn to love and accept yourself for who you are. Gratitude can help with that too.

You can be grateful for getting through the past 24 hours without a drink.

You can be grateful for your commitment to wanting to be a better person.

Remember to feel grateful for yourself, your achievements and your progress. You matter too!

You're prompted to note down three things you're grateful for so you can really think about what matters to you. You may start by listing out material things, but I encourage you to dig deeper and tap into the gratitude that flows from the soul. Compare being grateful for your lovely, shiny Rolex to being grateful for the work ethic your parents instilled in you to give you the drive to do well at work.

If you find it challenging to come up with things to be grateful for, you'll find a gratitude list in the Appendix that will give you plenty of ideas to build on. The important thing is you think carefully about what you're grateful for.

While you can use the same things every day if you really can't think of anything new, I would humbly suggest that if you do, you're copping out. You're going for the laziest route of least resistance, which means you won't get the full benefit of your gratitude practice. I strongly encourage you to come up with three new things every day. This will train your mind to think deeper about what you have to be genuinely grateful for. The more intensely you can feel gratitude, the more you'll experience stronger positive emotions, which can have a more significant impact on your overall happiness.

My sobriety today may be challenged by...

Now that we've explored your feelings and taken some time to sit in gratitude, the next step is to focus on your sobriety journey and what you can do to prepare yourself for another day without alcohol.

We're taking this day by day to keep things manageable. It's no use thinking ahead to tomorrow or next week when the overall goal is to stay sober today, so we only focus on today.

So, focus on this prompt:

My sobriety today may be challenged by:

1.

2.

3.

Consider any potential obstacles you may face in the next 24 hours that could challenge your sobriety. Maybe it's a day when you usually go for a drink with friends or workmates. Perhaps you know you've got a particularly stressful meeting coming up, and you would usually use alcohol as a crutch to get you through and/or reward yourself after. Conversely, you might have something to celebrate, like a birthday or wedding, and you would usually have a drink or eight to toast the occasion.

Whatever your triggers, this is where we will identify them (to help build your self-awareness) and plan ahead so you can avoid them or minimise their impact. After all, as they say, "fail to plan, and you plan to fail".

You'll be prompted to list out your coping strategies in the next section, but for now, just take a moment to think about what situations might come up today and start considering what alternative action you could take.

So, for example, you might be used to getting home from work and immediately cracking open a beer or pouring a glass of wine to unwind after a stressful day. Your main motive here is to relax and release that stress, so what could you do instead?

You might like to go to the gym and use exercise to work off that stress. You could go to the cinema and catch the latest release – wouldn't talking about a movie at work the next day be more interesting than how many beers you had the night before? You could meditate for twenty minutes when you get home to break the connection with drink and give your mind a break. You could go for a walk to explore your local park or discover your closest nature reserve.

It doesn't matter what you choose to do, so go for something that appeals to you, whether it's one of my suggestions or something completely different. The main focus is changing your habits to break the connection between a trigger and drinking and build new neural pathways focused on a healthier way of living.

We have added some examples in the Appendix to give you some ideas.

How can I stay sober today?

This is your final morning prompt and builds on the previous exercise.

You will be asked:

How can I stay sober today?

1.

2.

3.

These should answer the previous prompt and get you thinking ahead about potential obstacles and how to overcome them before they happen. We want to minimise surprises in your 31 days of completing this challenge, and this is a great practice to avoid them catching you off guard.

Some days will be more triggering than others, so you may find you don't need to think of as many coping strategies depending on what you've got going on. It could be something as simple as *don't buy alcohol when I do my weekly shop.* If you don't have alcohol in the house, it's much easier to choose to stay sober because you have to take conscious action to go out and get some.

These final two prompts are vital because they get you thinking about potential obstacles in advance and then develop personalised strategies to mitigate them. The more you practice this, the easier it will become to win the challenge and enjoy all the life-changing benefits of sobriety.

Stress is easily the number one reason why people fall off the wagon. If you're living a stressful lifestyle, think about whether there's anything you can do to reduce that stress.

Whatever your stress level, now's the time to learn healthier ways of dealing with it. With the best will in the world, you'll never be able to completely eliminate stress from your life, so what are you going to do about that doesn't involve drinking?

You can:

- Go to the gym.
- Get a personal trainer and commit to 8 sessions (start going on a triggering day like Friday night to counteract the "itch").
- Go for a walk.
- Get out in nature.
- Go to the cinema.
- Go bowling.
- Play golf (You have full permission to play every day if it keeps you sober – just think about breathing, eating and supporting your family as well though!)
- Meditate.
- Do yoga.
- Axe throwing
- Cooking that challenges you (beans on toast hardly takes much thought!)
- Dance.
- Go to individual therapy.
- Go to Alcoholics Anonymous and/or SMART Recovery group meetings (or other sober groups).
- Go to the theatre.

- Spend time with friends who can listen and support you.

These are all effective ways of naturally reducing stress (and double up as sober dating ideas!), and none of them come with a hangover and lousy mood the following morning.

Night Journal

We complete our journaling practice with four more prompts in the evening, ideally done last thing at night before you settle down to sleep.

This evening I feel...

This finishes the exercise you began in the morning by allowing you to reflect on how your emotions may have changed throughout the day and what precipitated those changes. Maybe you noticed a change in your thinking that had a corresponding knock-on effect on your emotions.

Do this exercise without judgement. You may have ended the day in a better mood than when you started, but it's also possible you wound up in a worse mood.

However you're feeling, simply accept it for what it is. There's no right or wrong way to feel, but when you become a conscious observer of yourself, you can notice your triggers and work with them to choose a different response in the future.

What could you have done better today?

Hindsight is 20/20. It's very easy to look back and think *if only...*

It's no use beating yourself up over your mistakes. In fact, mistakes are great. Mistakes are how we learn. But we can only learn if we take time out to consider what went wrong and what we can do differently when a similar situation occurs.

So, maybe you met with a friend for a coffee while you were on this sober journey, but they were doing what they always do and had a glass of wine or pint of beer. The feeling of "fuck it" was building the entire time, and you almost caved in and ordered that big glass of wine. This made you think about how tough it was to resist. Do you need to take some time out from seeing that friend until you're more confident about being around them while they continue to booze? Why couldn't they join you for a coffee instead of ordering a big glass of wine? Have you ever had a relationship with this person that hasn't been centred around alcohol?

Wherever you feel you could improve a situation throughout your day, think about alternative approaches for the future so you can make better choices.

Did you feel triggered to drink today? If so, what triggered you to think about drinking?

In the space below this prompt, explore the trigger in depth. Whether it's a new trigger you were unaware of or one you know is likely to be an issue, think about why that particular trigger had an effect on you. If you notice the same things coming up repeatedly, you could consider what extra strategies you can implement to help you deal with them.

You might also notice that as time goes on, you have fewer and fewer triggers to write about because you can go a whole day without needing a drink. This also gives you something to celebrate and is one reason why journaling is such a helpful tool. There might be times when you feel like your new lifestyle isn't making much of a difference, and this is human nature at play – we want everything to change immediately. If it was that easy, everyone would be sober, and I wouldn't need to produce this Challenge.

Understanding your triggers is hard work (compared to just getting drunk), and by doing this daily, you are building a more exciting future for yourself, so remember to push through those critical voices and keep going. You can look back over your journal notes and see just how far you've really come!

What did you do well today to maintain your sobriety?

While it's important to think about how we can improve on situations throughout the day, it's just as important to celebrate your wins. The more you give yourself a high five or pat on the back for those successes, no matter how small, the more you reinforce these new patterns of behaviour and motivate yourself to stick with them. It's basically the same as training a puppy to do the right thing at the right time – we want you to do the right thing for your sobriety at the right time, and the results in every area of your life will improve as a result.

For example, you could have identified in the last prompt that Jane triggered you at work today because of her attitude to other colleagues. Now, you are on the path to sober enlightenment; you stepped back from joining her in moaning about everyone and decided to keep your peace. The end result was not getting involved in someone else's drama, which could have triggered more emotions and led to you drinking.

Daily Reflections

In between your day and night journal, you'll find daily reflections based on the *Sober On A Drunk Planet* series. These are short reads you can dip into after you've finished your day journal prompts to inspire you to stay on track throughout the day. You might like to read them again at night to really get the messages and advice to stick.

These lessons are designed to give you insight and make you think differently. They will help you start taking positive action and build a strong connection with your intuition over the next 31 days to help you successfully complete this challenge.

Intentionally short and easily digested, they complement your journaling work and mean you shouldn't need more than ten minutes in the morning to start the day on a positive footing. They are designed to challenge you to consider how you think and whether that serves you; how you react emotionally and whether you need to make different choices; how you have ultimate control and responsibility over all your actions, even though tossing alcohol down your throat can seem like an involuntary reaction to life sometimes!

The "Question of the Day" at the end of the reading is designed to make you think about your relationship with alcohol in a way you might not have thought about previously. The questions are designed with a straightforward idea – "if it doesn't challenge you, it doesn't change you" – so if you think they are tough questions, it's a good sign because they challenge you to think differently.

Sobering Features – To Really Help You Win

While the journal prompts and lessons will go a long way towards supporting you to stay sober, I wanted to ensure you had everything you needed to help you make long-lasting changes to your lifestyle. So, I've included several additional features to equip you for the next 31 days and beyond.

Results are always a reflection of the effort you put in, so the more features you use, the greater self-awareness you can develop, the more positive action you will take, and the greater your overall intuition will develop.

Finance Tracker

Do you appreciate the true cost of your drinking? In this table, you'll be able to calculate how much you would have spent on alcohol in a week. At the end of the challenge, you'll find a final table that will allow you to calculate how much you're saving in a month, and then, you can use this figure to estimate how much you could save over 6 months, 5 years and 10 years.

Chasing money can be a toxic trait, and I know first-hand that money doesn't buy happiness; it is an essential part of living on this drunk planet. We can't avoid it. We all need money to survive (and to keep up those expensive CrossFit memberships), so it's worth knowing how much more of it you can have by quitting alcohol for good (and it will shock you!).

Fill in the table below with how much you would have spent had you gone out drinking this week. Be realistic and base it on what you would typically consume. Include any extras that might accompany a night out, such as food, takeaways, taxis, other drugs, etc. Equally, if you do most of your drinking in the house, write out all the associated costs of drinking at home.

Here's an example based on what a typical night out looked like for me before I got sober:

Item	Cost per drink/item	How many?	Total
Pint of beer	£5 ($7)	6	£30 (£42)
Glass of wine	£7 ($10)	3	£21 ($30)
Cocktail	£12 ($16)	3	£36 ($48)
Round of shots	£30 ($41)	1	£30 ($41)
Club entry	£20 ($27)	1	£20 ($27)
Gram of cocaine	£60 ($82)	2	£120 ($164)
Packet of cigarettes	£12 ($16)	2	£24 ($32)
Taxi home	£30 ($41)	1	£30 ($41)
Food (Before and after)	£30 ($41)	1	£30 ($41)
		Total	£341 ($466)

US Dollar costs are based on an approximate exchange rate of £1/$1.36. Everyone is different, and it doesn't matter whether you spend more or less than I did; it's all about the impact it has on your finances (not mine).

Now fill it out for yourself:

Item	Cost per drink/item	How many?	Total
		Total	

We will use the total number at the end of the Challenge to show you what you could do with that money rather than piss it all away (again).

Triggers (People, Places and Things)

Triggers are divided into three columns – *People, Places and Things*. As you develop your journaling process, you'll notice specific patterns accompanying your drinking. This is the place to record those observations so you can be more aware of situations that cause you to turn to a drink and plan what to do when faced with a trigger.

The idea is that we want to understand our triggers so we can combat them head-on before the trigger turns into an uncontrollable craving for alcohol, which might manifest itself as obsessing over alcohol and/or feelings of irritability. If you remain blind to your triggers, you will do what you always do and get drunk.

We are consciously trying to stop the cycle of:

Trigger > Crave > Drunk

While we can stop a trigger, we can also stop ourselves from craving alcohol, but these are harder to overcome initially, so we want to control the cycle at the first point if we can, e.g. the trigger.

The exercise will list People, Places and Things (including emotions) that can be triggering.

- **People.** These are the people who you're with when you have a drink or people who cause you to have a drink, e.g. someone has pissed you off at work. Note down why that person has triggered you, e.g., my boss gave me a bad review at work and I feel useless, or my mate Alan invited me out for some beers, but that always turns into coming home two days later.
- **Places.** These are the places where you usually drink. It could be a pub or bar, but it could also be your home (and note down the rooms where you tend to drink), your office or a friend's home. Make detailed notes on what it is about this place that causes you to drink. For example, when I go to the local pub/bar, I see the same people moaning about the same things, which triggers me to drink.
- **Things (including emotions).** This column is for anything else that isn't a person or place but has you turning to drink. It could be a particular set of

circumstances, such as a party or special event, or it could be a particular smell that reminds you of being abroad that you heavily associate with drinking (yes, triggers can be anything!). This is the place to put certain emotions down, such as happiness, anger and sadness, that are triggers to drink. Go into as much detail as possible about why you think this is a trigger.

At the moment, your brain contains neural pathways that have built a connection between a trigger, e.g. your boss telling you that you aren't performing well enough, which triggers an emotion that you don't understand (yet), which then starts the process of you craving alcohol because you've done it so many times in the past.

Our brains have a feature called neuroplasticity, which means that however old you are or how engrained a habit is, you can always develop new neural pathways supporting new behaviour patterns. At first, it can be challenging to do something different when faced with a trigger. Still, the more you become self-aware of your triggers, the more you can change your reactions and the stronger the new neural pathways develop, which means new, healthier choices will start to happen on auto-pilot (just like getting drunk once used to).

Write down your list of triggers and continually add to them as you complete the next 31 days, as understanding these is a vital tool for becoming Sober On A Drunk Planet.

People	Places	Things

(Continued in the Appendix)

Sober Accountability

Set yourself up for success with an accountability buddy.
Even better, get lots of accountability buddies!

Join the Sober On A Drunk Planet Community and put up
a post introducing yourself, saying you're starting your 31-
day journal and explaining why you want to do it. If you
feel too shy now, join and read posts, listen to podcasts
and find your way around while building up your sober
days. You will know when you feel ready to start sharing.

Accountability is one of the most successful tools for
getting results. Just think about any exercise class you
have done – would you have put that much effort in if you
did it alone? Getting sober on your own is hard, but being
around others fighting the same fight makes life easier,
and when you share a common goal, it's a beautiful group
to be in (unless it's CrossFit – then you are just mad and
enjoy pain).

The group helps keep the group sober, and that's
powerful. The more you own up to your truth around
alcohol and feel comfortable sharing those truths with
like-minded people (yes, we are all equally crazy and have
horrific stories to share about our drinking days), the

easier it gets – it's a form of group therapy. I highly recommend you join us so we can share in your success and help you with your struggles.

Use the QR code below to join:

Or visit:

www.soberonadrunkplanet.com/community

In addition to our community, there are plenty of other amazing communities out there, and it's a case of trying them all to find the ones that fit with you. Always try to look at the similarities and not the differences, especially if you go to in-person groups because we are all crazy; it just depends on what level of crazy you feel comfortable around.

Be Inspired

One of the most significant tools to my own recovery, and for millions of others, is when you listen to someone's story about what their drinking (and/or drugging) looked like and how sobriety has completely turned their life around. It gives you hope that you are not alone and that sobriety really is the best thing that could ever happen to you.

It shows you that it can be done. It shows you that people in worse positions have got sober, got out of debt, repaired their broken family, got promoted at work, left prison a reformed person and achieved anything you can think of! Sobriety is one of the most potent lifestyles you can follow on a planet obsessed with getting drunk, and each of the podcast guests re-affirms that belief.

The guests on the podcasts all have unique stories, which might be the story you can relate to the most. It might just be that podcast you needed to hear to keep you sober.

All this time, you might have thought you were the only person in the world with these challenges to overcome, but I can assure you, there are millions of people like you – you just have to be prepared to listen.

My suggestion is that you use these podcasts to help hit home the message of sobriety. You will learn lots of new information in these podcasts, be inspired and hopefully use what you learn in your own journey.

The best part is you can use these podcasts at times when you might be triggered to drink and use them as a way to dull out the irritability and restlessness of wanting that drink. The craving will pass, and you can get back to filling in your triggers list.

You can access the podcast using the QR code below:

Or visit:

www.soberonadrunkplanet.com/podcasts

Additional Reading/Listening Materials

If you want to understand the tools and processes as you work your way through this challenge, you can check out our international bestselling books below:

If you want to understand more about the tools to stop drinking and take a deeper dive around the '3 Sober Steps' mentioned, order '*3 Sober Steps*' today by using the QR code below:

Or visit www.soberonadrunkplanet.com/books

If you want to re-affirm why you are doing the sober thing and need a reminder about the benefits of long-term sobriety and what your future could look like without alcohol - Check out the International Bestseller – '*Giving Up Alcohol*' - using the QR code below:

Or visit www.soberonadrunkplanet.com/books

We encourage you to read/listen to as many sobriety and self-help books as possible. Books/audiobooks are one of the greatest returns on investments you can ever make!

For access to our mailing list and free E-book (7 Sober Secrets You Can't Ignore), with our sometimes weekly, sometimes sporadic but normally on Friday afternoons, Friday Ramble Email, which is a collection of thoughts to help keep you sober, use the QR code below:

Or visit www.soberonadrunkplanet.com/free-resources/#7SoberSecrets

The purpose of these regular email communications is to keep sobriety top of mind and help you focus on your goal of staying sober.

#Transformationtuesday

It's insane how much people change physically when they give up alcohol, and it's certainly worth taking a selfie now (or keeping a recent photo) so you can keep it for your future #transformationtuesday photo!

Results will vary from person to person; some take weeks, and others take months to notice those changes. The only goal that matters at this stage is to stay sober.

A reminder about fitness: the internal benefits of exercise that keep us stronger and fitter, both physically and mentally, are the real end goals of giving up alcohol.

Yes, sobriety can make some of us unbearable with how proud we are of our own transformations! But remember, looking good is great, just don't be a dick about it when it happens!

This is your cue to take that photo now or dig out that horrific selfie that's still on your camera roll from your last horrendous hangover. Even if you can't find a photo or don't dare to take one now, Facebook memories won't take long to give you lots of options to save (I still get shocking reminders about how bad my drinking was even today).

Appendix

In the appendix, you'll find a few useful tools to help with your journaling. I've included the Emotions Wheel, a suggested list of things to be grateful for, examples of potential threats to your sobriety, and examples of solutions to those threats. There is an additional table to add more resentments; you will get to this exercise in one of your day reflections. If you are like me, by the time I gave up drinking, I resented a lot of people and needed a lot of writing space to let them go.

Make A Promise

In my experience, people without a why end up following other people and, therefore live lives dictated by other people. This challenge is designed to ignite that fire within you so you can move from being the passenger to the driver in your own story.

When we move from being the passenger to the driver, we must take control of how that train is driven, and that requires a lot of fuel (assuming we are on a steam train, which isn't the best for the environment I know, but you hopefully get the idea). Having a strong why is that fuel that will keep burning strong, even when you have off days and it allows you to keep going forward, no matter what. You are responsible for your motivation, starting with a strong why – now's your time to find it.

Just as an example, I made a promise to myself after another New Year's Eve that basically saw me reach my newest rock bottom of being completely broken (financially, emotionally, mentally, spiritually and physically). I reached my "sober tipping point" and the pain of having another pint or doing another line of coke was far greater than getting sober. Sobriety, by this point, was the only choice I wanted to make as I was sick and tired of feeling sick and tired.

I promised myself that morning that if I put half the effort into my recovery as I did in finding drugs and getting blind drunk (having once travelled 3 hours to get drugs before a business meeting), then I would have a marvellous life. That's the promise I have kept to myself to this day, and the image of me in the flat curled up and crying is as clear as anything. I don't recognise that person anymore, but I am forever grateful to my former self for keeping that promise.

Now it's time for you to think about your why.

Why are you doing this sobriety journal?

What do you want life to look like for you?

What are you hoping to get from sobriety that alcohol hasn't delivered?

Think about these answers for a few moments because these will get that fire burning inside of you (and it might take a period of sobriety to get to that point).

Use this space to write a promise to yourself (maybe practice on a separate writing pad first) so you can look back at why you are starting this in the first place. It can be a few words, a few sentences or a book series – whatever works for you now (but ideally long enough to fit in the space below).

Once you have made your promise, it will be time to get started – sobriety is one of the most powerful gifts you can give yourself, so for 31 days, give this your full attention and take it each day at a time – You can do it and become Sober On A Drunk Planet!

I promise myself........

(Use this space below to make that promise)

The Challenge Begins

Day 1

Morning Journal

Today I feel:

I am grateful for:

1.

2.

3.

My sobriety today may be challenged by:

1.

2.

3.

How can I stay sober today?

1.

2.

3.

Day 1 - Sober Goals – The Importance of 24 Hours

Think of yourself as dead. You have lived your life. Now take what's left and live it properly – Marcus Aurelius.

A therapy technique you can use to shock yourself into sobriety is to write your own eulogy (the speech someone says about the person who died at a funeral). What would it look like if you were to write a eulogy for your life to this day? Would you be proud of it? Would you think it was a waste of life?

The chances are, you are here because of the destructive nature of alcohol, and you have fallen out of love with what you see in the mirror – if you did an eulogy today, it would probably reflect that.

Luckily, sobriety gives you all the time, energy and money you need to change that narrative and re-write the most epic eulogy, which will hopefully be much further down the road now that you are no longer poisoning yourself with alcohol (that's literally what it does!).

This journal is your chance to help you start re-writing your future so you can take back control of what that future looks like – not carrying on being a slave to alcohol, which destroys your time, energy and money (the polar opposite of sobriety).

And goals are a big part of achieving. If you can see it, you can achieve it, and millions of people have already walked the same walk as you (some of which are in the Sober On A Drunk Planet Community if you need some inspiration) and have transformed their lives beyond their wildest dreams.

Your goal with this journal is to stay sober for 31 days. Right now, that might seem like an impossible dream, but what if I told you that didn't have to be your goal right now?

What if you just made your goal to stay sober for the next 24 hours?

Goals don't have to be big and grandiose. They can be small or short-term. But don't underestimate the importance of those little goals – a lot of the time, those small goals lay the foundations for hitting the bigger ones. A goal of staying sober for 24 hours is a crucial first step towards a bigger goal of staying sober for a week, which is another step towards the even bigger goal of staying sober for a month.

If you've been to support groups, you've probably learnt about the "just for today" mindset. Alcoholics Anonymous members keep a keyring or coin with them inscribed with this mantra to remind them that you only have to take things one day at a time. Keep your energy focused on what's happening right now rather than worrying about the future or beating yourself up about the past.

When you achieve a goal, even a little one, you feel positive about yourself and trigger a healthy feedback loop. It's like deciding to clean your bathroom sink and then end up scrubbing the whole room because you love how the sink looks, and it feels good to have a clean bathroom? Or it could just be my OCD.

Start with 24 hours. Achieve that and use the positive feeling you get from that one positive action to drive you on to the next 24 hours and the next. Give yourself a reward for doing so well – just don't make it an alcoholic drink!

Up until now, you've been using drink to reward yourself, no matter what the circumstances. Feeling happy?

Celebrate it with a drink! Feeling down? Cheer yourself up with a drink! When you've associated the entire wheel of emotions with a drink, no wonder drink automatically becomes your first choice when you want to reward yourself for reaching a goal. When you recognise that connection and take active steps to choose a different reward, you start changing your brain's wiring and build healthier reward habits.

If rewarding yourself is a trigger, add it to the triggers list at the front of this book under 'things'. For example, I reward myself with a drink when I do well at work.

If you've read *3 Sober Steps,* you will have learned about the SMART way to set goals.

SMART stands for:

- SPECIFIC
- MEASURABLE
- ACHIEVABLE
- REALISTIC
- TIME-BOUND

How would this look when setting sober goals?

SPECIFIC:

Stop drinking alcohol for 24 hours. This is a much more powerful goal than simply saying you're going to stop drinking. It's a clear goal, and you'll know if you've accomplished it.

MEASURABLE:

Measuring your alcohol intake (or lack of it) allows you to build upon your progress. It's easy to see whether you've drunk anything or not.

You might like to set in place accountability strategies, like joining an online or offline sobriety group, track your progress on a sobriety app, and/or work with a therapist/counsellor.

ACHIEVABLE:

Giving up drinking IS achievable. I did it, countless others did it, and you can too. That's not to say it'll be easy, but it's definitely something you can achieve.

REALISTIC:

Is it realistic to think you can stay sober? Absolutely! The fact you've started this journal is a demonstration of your commitment. You've got this!

TIME-BOUND:

A goal of being sober for 24 hours isn't overwhelming when compared to being sober for 31 days. And when you break down what 24 hours actually looks like, you should be asleep for around eight hours, working for the same amount of time and only have eight hours left. Essentially, we need to avoid drinking at work (which can be a trigger if you drink at lunch, during or after work) and during our eight hours of free time (it will be much less if you have kids!). I haven't met anyone yet who manages to drink whilst asleep, so I always suggest that sleeping more is a good thing when trying to give up alcohol, as it's a safe space to stay sober.

A journey of 1000 miles begins with a single step. Your journey to sobriety starts with a single, alcohol-free day.

I have goals for all areas of my life, and they give me a strong sense of purpose, a purpose I could never find in a bottle or cocaine packet, no matter how hard I looked.

For now though, you need to focus all your energy on getting through each day sober. Everything you do should focus on maintaining that goal each day, so cancel any other big plans as they will add unnecessary stress to achieving that goal. You need to become as narrow-minded about sobriety as you did about drinking!

Top Tip: Your first goal is to stay sober for the next 24 hours. Every time you feel tempted to do something that might get you drinking, ask yourself:

"Will my actions move me towards or away from my goal today?"

This will give you a moment to consider the consequences of your choices. Some people call it "playing the tape forward". What usually happens if you have a drink? Remember how that hangover feels? The sense of that horrible headache and dry mouth feeling you always get from getting drunk. You can effectively repeat any of your previous drinking nights out and see how you fared the day after – because history DOES repeat itself when it comes to drinking alcohol.

Remember why you started this journey and start to develop healthier habits instead of acting on your old drinking autopilot.

Evening Journal

This evening I feel:

What could you have done better today?

Did you feel triggered to drink today? If so, what triggered you to think about drinking?

What did you do well today to maintain your sobriety?

Day 2

Morning Journal

Today I feel:

I am grateful for:

1.

2.

3.

My sobriety today may be challenged by:

1.

2.

3.

How can I stay sober today?

1.

2.

3.

Day 2: Sober Self-Awareness For The Currently Unaware

Know thyself - Socrates

The only way you'll be able to be sober long term is by educating yourself on yourself and by understanding the real truth about alcohol. Maybe you already know some of this, but this hasn't been enough to motivate you to stop.

That's why you need to dig deeper into why you drink the way you do (potentially with the help of a good therapist) and identify your past patterns surrounding alcohol so you can consciously change them.

Right now, you may not have a clue why you continue to drink, even though you know it's not good for you. That's okay. Plenty of people struggle with self-awareness. You can probably think of a few examples in your social and work circles of people who do things yet are oblivious to their impact on those around them. You could maybe even say what they should be doing differently and wonder why they don't.

It's hard to look yourself in the mirror and be honest about what you see. It'll be well worth it, but it does take courage. It's certainly not something you can do while under the influence of alcohol or trying to push through a hangover.

Self-awareness is one of the most powerful tools in your battle against the control alcohol has over you. As Viktor Frankl put it, "Between stimulus and response, there is a space. In that space lies our freedom and power to choose our response. In our response lies our growth and freedom."

The journal prompts will help you develop your emotional intelligence to create more 'space' and take more positive actions towards staying sober.

There are countless 'stimuli' that can be the trigger for a drink. A hard day at work. A relationship ending. Going on a date. A hot summer's day. Celebrating or commiserating your team's performance at a game. A wedding, funeral, birthday, Christmas and stag/hen party.

Yet none of these things *have* to lead to the 'response' of drinking (yes, you can do stag/hen parties sober!). Plenty of people don't drink in response to bad news and find other ways to celebrate the good things in life.

So what has you reaching for a drink, and why? Is it anxiety? Is it a feeling of not being good enough? Do you feel left out if you don't drink? Is it a trauma that keeps bringing you back to the bottle? Is it just a habit, or are you addicted? Is alcohol *really* the only thing that will do at that moment?

Once you learn how bad alcohol actually is, you can't unlearn it. It then raises the question of why do you REALLY drink the poisonous drug alcohol? What are you trying to escape from?

If you start opening yourself up to the alternatives, you start recognising that what you thought about alcohol may not be the universal truth you believed it was.

I used to think that alcohol made me more attractive to the opposite sex and gave me the confidence to be charming and charismatic. If I'd been honest with myself, I could have acknowledged that was far from the truth. In fact, I was perpetually single for most of my twenties!

I thought alcohol was harmless to my health but the high blood pressure, irritable bowel syndrome, depression and all the associated diseases with being overweight were only made evident when they all disappeared after I stopped drinking alcohol.

Alcohol is a poison and addictive drug, and to think of it any other way is fake news.

It's time to challenge your established beliefs around drinking and change them to something that not only reflects reality but also supports your new sober lifestyle. It's time to read those Sober On A Drunk Planet books that detail the damage alcohol has been doing to your mind and body. It's time to open up those scary bank statements and see how much money you've lost to drinking and its associated expenses. It might be time to finally get guidance from a therapist/counsellor who can help you heal.

It's time to be honest with yourself about the values you want to live by and start making it happen.

The question below is designed to get you thinking differently outside of your drunk mind and into your new sober mind. To help you create more 'space' so you can make better 'responses' to staying sober. Have a think throughout the day and come back to these tonight before you do your evening journal.

"What's really going on for me when I decide to get drunk?"

It can be deeply revealing when you answer this question honestly. It can also be painful and bring up all sorts of difficult emotions. But they will help you develop greater self-awareness and set you on the road to change.

Journal Space To Write

Journal Space To Write

Evening Journal

This evening I feel:

What could you have done better today?

Did you feel triggered to drink today? If so, what triggered you to think about drinking?

What did you do well today to maintain your sobriety?

Day 3

Morning Journal

Today I feel:

I am grateful for:

1.

2.

3.

My sobriety today may be challenged by:

1.

2.

3.

How can I stay sober today?

1.

2.

3.

Day 3: Understanding Your Triggers And Cravings

Failing to plan is planning to fail.

How many times have you decided to quit drinking only for something to happen that made you go *"fuck it"* and reach for the nearest beer?

If you've been drinking for a while, you'll find yourself craving alcohol. This is because alcohol triggers the release of dopamine, that feel-good hormone that can also be generated by exercise, sex, food, going shopping, or doing anything you find pleasurable. However, alcohol gradually lowers your natural dopamine levels, so your brain craves alcohol to get that rush of hormones to feel good. This is why so many of us turn to alcohol as a pick-me-up.

Triggers aren't the same as cravings, but they're what lead to them. Triggers can be all manner of things, from being around certain people, being in particular places, or everyday things. They can even be seemingly random things like a smell or memory. Cravings are when you develop an obsession and/or irritability/itch that you NEED a drink. Sometimes referred to as the "Wine Witch" or "Beer Beelzebub" (I made the last one up), that explains a nagging voice on your shoulder trying to convince you to just have one drink.

For example, that "Friday Night Feeling" is a deep, intense craving triggered by all the people, places and things that have triggered you up to that moment. Friends texting you about the weekend, colleagues talking about their boozy weekend plans, a message from the drug dealer saying, "3 for 100," and the fact that work has been stressful all week all trigger you to that intense craving. You are ITCHING to get drunk to release that overwhelming irritability that has been triggered by everything to that point – the "Friday Night Feeling". This is a challenging situation – you want to drink, but you also want to honour your commitment to sobriety. The "Friday Night Feeling" can turn into the "Every Night Feeling" if alcohol really gets its claws into you.

This is where becoming self-aware of your triggers is crucial so you can take action to stay sober. Just the thought of a night on the town can be enough to release that dopamine rush, making you want to experience even more of those positive feelings and giving you a craving for alcohol.

It's time to break the connection between drinking alcohol and your specific triggers. Initially, you need to avoid those triggers and reward your healthy new behaviours so you can develop new neural pathways supporting your sobriety. You might need to avoid certain social situations, to begin with, but if anyone gives you grief about this, remind yourself that those who matter won't mind, and those who mind don't matter.

Here are some common triggers. How many do you recognise in yourself? Use the space below to explore and identify your triggers.

- People
    - Drinking buddies
    - Family members
    - Difficult colleagues
    - Drinking co-workers
    - Book club
    - Sports team
- Places
    - Pubs

- o Clubs

- o Holidays

- o Sports venues

- o Funerals

- o Weddings

- o Friends' houses

- Things

  - o The smell of alcohol

  - o Cigarettes

  - o Pint glasses

  - o Wine glasses

  - o Online food shop

  - o Friday Nights

  - o Thursday Nights

  - o Every day that ends with day?!

  - o Hot weather

  - o Cold weather

  - o Wet weather (Or cold, wet and dark weather if you are living through a British winter) o Video games

o Certain times of the day or week

o Songs

o Change of seasons

Use this time to add any triggers to your own list and regularly revisit your list as you uncover more things that lead to you craving a drink. Remember to keep adding to your list at the front of the book to create a conscious list of all those things to avoid and/or plan around.

Evening Journal

This evening I feel:

What could you have done better today?

Did you feel triggered to drink today? If so, what triggered you to think about drinking?

What did you do well today to maintain your sobriety?

Day 4

Morning Journal

Today I feel:

I am grateful for:

1.

2.

3.

My sobriety today may be challenged by:

1.

2.

3.

How can I stay sober today?

1.

2.

3.

Day 4: Dealing With Triggers And Cravings – The Big Red Fuck It Button (Version 2.0)

If you hang around the barbers long enough, you will eventually get a haircut.

Once you know your triggers, start considering how you will mitigate them. If you have an event coming up that you know will involve alcohol, visualising and planning ahead will help you cope. Find out what non-alcoholic drinks will be available and have an exit strategy if it gets too much.

It's important to state that while we are trying to avoid triggers to avoid cravings for alcohol, we can't always prevent the cravings. Even after long spells of sobriety, people can have an intense craving for alcohol when there has been no obvious trigger. So, we have to manage the cravings as well as we do the triggers because cravings require a more immediate solution, and we have to overcome that craving before it turns into a glass of alcohol. The options to help overcome cravings are highlighted further down, but the main difference is that the craving will require an immediate solution in order to NOT pick up that drink.

There is a magic button that you can use.

Rather than go to these events and hit the "big red fuck it" button where you go all in and come home 3 days later regretting every decision you have ever made. Change the narrative of what that button can do for you in sobriety.

I still have a "fuck it" button. But that button is now a button to "get the fuck out of the place I am in so I can go home, go to bed and maintain my sobriety and inner peace". The newly programmed "big red fuck it" button version 2.0 gives me permission to leave straight away. The process of having to move in order to leave will get me out of my own head space and away from everything that is triggering me. Movement is a great medicine for curing obsessiveness and irritability when it comes to alcohol.

So while you might associate the "big red fuck it" button with getting shit-faced and ruining the rest of your week/weekend – sobriety allows you to hold onto the button. You just need to re-programme it to suit your new lifestyle and help you avoid triggers and cravings. The goal is to avoid that first drink at all costs, and this new style of "fuck it" helps achieve that.

So, if you want, you can use this button anytime over the next 31 days and beyond to help you get back to a safe place, away from those triggers and cravings that might make you want to drink.

The Big Red Fuck It Button Version 2.0 – Yes, this is a black button and not a Red button as stated, but colour printing is EXPENSIVE!

(Go on – Push it ;)

With the best will in the world, it's hard to avoid all your triggers all the time. Even after years of sobriety, I still find myself being triggered sometimes. Even a simple shopping trip or visit to the gym can see me bump into drug dealers I used to know and old drinking friends whom I have awkwardly avoided since getting sober. The difference is that I now have the tools to make better choices.

It's really important that you still look at how you can avoid your triggers. Take different routes to avoid going past the places you associate with drink. Suggest going to a coffee shop rather than a pub, and if your friends aren't happy about it, consider making new friends! When you no longer have to confine yourself to places that serve alcohol, you'll be surprised at just how many choices you have.

In the early stages, the simplest way to handle triggers is to say NO to triggering situations. Once you've been sober for a while, you can start going back to them slowly to begin with, e.g. don't finish this Challenge, then treat yourself to an all-inclusive break to Cancun during Spring Break!

If in doubt, don't go because when you are ready, you won't even doubt your decision (remember to listen to your gut!).

Here are some strategies to help you cope with triggers and cravings:

- Build a support network online with the Sober On A Drunk Planet Community
- Attend in-person and online meetings through AA/SMART recovery plus other sober groups (there are plenty of great sober communities to choose from). Surround yourself with people who are happy to help you stay sober when you're struggling.
- When you feel a craving, become self-aware of it. Try to change what you are doing so your physiology changes your internal chemistry, and your focus will shift. Some people would suggest "urge surfing", which is sitting with that craving until it passes, but if you are newly sober, then it's likely you will say "fuck it" in a version 1.0 way because you haven't had time to practice. Instead, try moving about. Movement is medicine, and it doesn't have to be 200 burpees, 200 overhead presses and 1000km on the rowing machine like some CrossFit nutter; it can just be a short walk.
- Remember your why and look at your promise to yourself at the beginning of this Challenge. What made you want to get sober? You might like to list your reasons and keep them on your phone or in your bag so you can refer to them when you're

craving. Go back to your promise to yourself at the beginning of this book and keep it fresh in your thoughts which will ultimately impact your actions (in a positive way).

- Distract yourself. What can you do to divert your attention away from drink? Gym? Spin Class? Boxing class? CrossFit?! Read a Sober On A Drunk Planet book? Listen to the Podcast? Ask for help from others in the online group?

- Think it through and play the tape forward (you have a whole history to look back on – and yes, history repeats itself with drinking). When you tell yourself you're just going to have one or two, think about what will happen later. How will you feel tomorrow when you're hungover? How will you feel having broken your sober streak?

- Leave if you have to. If a situation is too hard, remove yourself from temptation and get out. Press that newly programmed "fuck it" button and protect your sobriety at all costs (it will get easier with time)!

For example, I used to crave alcohol/drugs around 10pm every night, so my fail-safe was to go to bed around 8.30pm and listen to self-help audiobooks. This was one of the life-changing habits I got into – listening to positive stories about people and their extraordinary lives and learning new ways to live and achieve my own dreams. When you swap late nights partying with early nights filled with learning new things – life changes very drastically and in a positive way.

I still go to bed at this time, listen to audiobooks (even though I think I have completed Audible) and wake up fresh after eight hours of sleep so I can get on doing what I want to do – something I am truly grateful for.

Action for the day – Write out a list of reasons why you want to be sober.

Take a photo of that list and keep it on your phone. Along with the selfie you might have taken a few days ago, you can use this list and the photo to constantly remind yourself why you are doing this. Re-reading your promise is another good reminder of why you are here.

Journal Space To Write

Evening Journal

This evening I feel:

What could you have done better today?

Did you feel triggered to drink today? If so, what triggered you to think about drinking?

What did you do well today to maintain your sobriety?

Day 5

Morning Journal

Today I feel:

I am grateful for:

1.

2.

3.

My sobriety today may be challenged by:

1.

2.

3.

How can I stay sober today?

1.

2.

3.

Day 5: Sober Energy vs Drunk Energy - Becoming a Sober Jedi

Where attention goes, energy flows – James Redfield.

Take a moment to do an honest assessment of yourself. When you're hungover, how easy is it to perform? How much energy can you give? 50%? 40%? More like 30%, right?

Now think about how many hangovers do you suffer in a week? 2? 3? 5? 7? And how may days does it take you to fully recover before you feel 100% again? You might not even know what 100% feels like if you've only known drinking from a young age and have always gone from feeling okay to being hungover again – this is your chance to find out what running at 100% feels like for the first time!

If you've heard of vibrational energy, you might have dismissed it as just New Age woo woo. However, it is increasingly recognised that vibrational medicine, or energy medicine to call it by another name, has a solid basis in scientific reality and offers a wealth of support to anyone wanting to improve their health and overall well-being. This includes getting and staying sober.

We are all made from particles that are constantly vibrating and generating energy. This means we all have our own energy field – it's just physics! You only need to be near someone's magnetic field to get a vibe from them (good, bad or indifferent).

We can find the concept of energy and vibration in various spiritual practices dating back to ancient times. Practices like Chinese medicine, yoga, chakra work, Qigong, feng shui, reiki, sound healing and acupuncture are all based on vibrational energy. And if you're sceptical about the efficacy of these practices, plenty of scientific studies show they work. Reiki has even been used in hospitals around the world as an effective form of pain relief and a way to promote healing.

Energy healers claim that we can speed up or slow down the vibration of our cells depending on what we think, how we behave and where we are. Changing your vibration naturally attracts positive or negative experiences.

If you're still dubious, think about these situations where energy is clearly at work:

- Hanging out with certain people leaves you feeling drained, and you can't explain why. These people are known as "Energy Vampires" – they will drain the life out of you with their problems and negative attitudes.

- Listening to certain songs can dramatically affect your mood, putting a smile on your face or facilitating an emotional release so you can finally cry. Even if it isn't your style of music, try listening to "Clarity" by Zedd and notice any changes in your mood. By doing this, you become aware of how vibrations impact your mood. And if you have never tried it, go to a sound healing or sound bath near you – that will change how you see the power of vibrations forever.

- Walking into a room, you instantly know the people there have had an argument, even though no one says a word. You are feeling the "vibe of the room", and it's not good!

We are energetic beings with an innate ability to detect and absorb the surrounding energy.

Proponents of vibrational energy hold that some people, places, feelings, and things have a low vibrational energy while others have a high vibrational energy. So-called negative emotions such as anger, fear, worry, and stress are all low vibrations, while feelings of peace, joy, love, and gratitude are all high vibrations.

If you want to support your new sober lifestyle, you should aim to build a life surrounded by lots of high vibe energy and avoid the low energies as much as possible.

As with so many of the techniques in this journal, self-awareness is key. The more you become conscious of how everything affects your energy, the more you can make high vibrational choices to support the life you want.

Remember your last hangover. (You probably don't have to think too hard!) That's the epitome of negative, low-vibe energy.

Most habitual drinkers tend to be low vibe. While they may be perfectly decent people, there'll be a reason why they drink so much, such as unresolved trauma or a deep unhappiness with their life, no matter how good it looks on the surface.

Compare what you feel like the morning after a drinking session to how you feel when you go to an exercise class, spend time in nature or take time out for your hobbies. It's a much better feeling, isn't it? You're filled with high-vibration energy, nourishing your soul, giving your body the chance to move, and soaking up positive energy from the happy people around you.

Choosing sobriety allows you to understand yourself and your energy levels so you can start choosing supportive, high-energy activities, places, and people. It's a very different feeling being surrounded by sober people all working on being their best selves to hanging out with other drinkers, often complaining about how hard done by they are or judging others (I used to do this all the time).

Here are a few ways you can actively raise your vibration:

- Seek out positive people who are also on a journey of self-discovery and personal growth. As you get sober, you may find some friends fall by the wayside. This is an opportunity to find new friends that will have a positive impact on your own energy.
- Hang out in positive places that make you feel good, like the gym, the cinema, the theatre, the park, and the homes of good friends and family.

- Exercise. Regular exercise makes you feel more energetic, even if you expend energy during an exercise class. And yes, the hardest lift of all is lifting your butt off the couch. Nobody has ever regretted a gym session or moving in some way to overcome a bad mood. It works, and it's 100% free for you to use as a great tool in sobriety.

- Eat nutritious food to fuel your energy from the inside. If you have ever eaten takeaway food for a prolonged period compared to eating healthy food, the difference in energy levels and mood is eye-opening!

- Go to classes focused on energy healing or book healing sessions. You might enjoy reiki, sound healing, or yoga. Give it a try at least once – you'll be amazed at how it can shift energy blocks you didn't even know existed.

- Spend time in nature - every day if you can.

- Go on sober holidays to take a break from the daily grind and refresh and rejuvenate your energy.

- Work on being more mindful and present in the moment.

- Avoid 'Energy Vampires'. Protect and grow your energy at all costs!

- Find a hobby that lights you up, and make time for it. Maybe you might like to do something you enjoyed as a child but have let slide over the years. Go to a dance class, learn a martial art, do cross stitch, climb a mountain or play the best sport in the world, golf ;) – whatever will make your soul sing!

The more you choose high-vibe activities, the better you'll feel. The more aware you become of your energy, the more you'll listen to your intuition when turning down invitations to events that will leave you feeling drained and dejected afterwards. You can check in with yourself whenever you're faced with a choice and question which one will take you closer to your sober goals and which will undermine them.

The more you work with your energies, the more you'll become a Sober Jedi. Where your attention goes, energy flows. Focus your attention on being sober, and the results will speak for themselves.

Do you want to look back at your life knowing you only gave it 30%, or would you like to feel proud that you gave it as close to 100% every day as possible?

Question for the day - Think of people you hang around for prolonged periods at work, in social situations and any hobby/sport you might do with others.

Think about people in those situations who make you feel good about yourself and leave you feeling happy.

And think about those people who make you feel worse about yourself and leave you feeling drained.

This practice will help you become more conscious of how other people and their energy impact you.

Become mindful of it and avoid negative energy for prolonged periods.

Journal Space To Write

Journal Space To Write

Evening Journal

This evening I feel:

What could you have done better today?

Did you feel triggered to drink today? If so, what triggered you to think about drinking?

What did you do well today to maintain your sobriety?

Day 6

Morning Journal

Today I feel:

I am grateful for:

1.

2.

3.

My sobriety today may be challenged by:

1.

2.

3.

How can I stay sober today?

1.

2.

3.

Day 6: FOMO vs JOMO

If in doubt, don't go out.

You've probably heard of FOMO – the Fear of Missing Out. I want to introduce you to JOMO - the Joy of Missing Out. FOMO's more self-aware cousin.

Fear is a powerful emotion. It can drive us to do all sorts of things we wouldn't do otherwise if we were thinking clearly.

But before you let FOMO send you out on another session, ask yourself, what are you really missing out on? Forgetting what you said and to whom and then worrying whether you put your foot in it? The hangover? The overspending? The goal you failed to reach because alcohol took over?

What if you let JOMO take the reins? You'll wake up tomorrow morning knowing exactly what happened, secure in the knowledge you didn't embarrass yourself. You're awake at a decent hour feeling clear-headed and ready to tackle the day head-on. Your bank balance is still healthy, leaving you with more money to spend on what you want. You've got the energy and drive to do whatever you want, whether it's doing something to further your career or doing something for the sheer enjoyment of it.

Both FOMO and JOMO set up feedback loops. You don't need me to tell you which one is better.

As you become more confident in setting boundaries, saying "no" when needed, and taking control of your life, you'll find yourself heading in new, exciting directions.

Remember, just because you're not drinking doesn't mean you have to stay home or stop having fun. It's just that you get to choose to go out because you want to rather than because you feel pressured or you'll miss out on something. And if you are out and about and feel like you need to go home immediately – press that newly programmed "fuck it, I want to protect my peace and sobriety, so I am outta here" button.

Don't be afraid to do what's right for you, even if you get pushback from those around you. This isn't their journey. It's yours, and you get to put yourself first.

Focus on the positive feedback you've received from making better choices. Think about how great you felt having no hangovers for the last five days. Remind yourself that you want to feel that great again and again and again.......

To help overcome FOMO, the biggest sobriety lesson I can share is this:
People do NOT care about you as much as you think they do. If they want to go out drinking, they will find someone to go with, regardless of your choice to say NO and put clear boundaries in place.

The friends that don't mind matter, and the friends that mind don't matter.

If in doubt, don't go out. This doesn't mean you can't enjoy staying in either, but if you want something different (sobriety), then you have to do something different (not go to the pub for 31 days).

Your confidence will naturally develop to a point where you know when the time is right, and it's highly likely, with all the time, money and energy you will create, that going to the pub for eight hours is no longer a priority.

Question for the day – Write down your biggest fears about getting sober.

Use this question to help open up about what fear really means for you in the context of giving up alcohol. You might like to share those fears in the online group and find out what other people's experiences are when they go through the first few months of sobriety.

If you want to share, use the QR code below:

Or visit:

www.soberonadrunkplanet.com/community

Journal Space To Write

Journal Space To Write

Evening Journal

This evening I feel:

What could you have done better today?

Did you feel triggered to drink today? If so, what triggered you to think about drinking?

What did you do well today to maintain your sobriety?

Day 7

Morning Journal

Today I feel:

I am grateful for:

1.

2.

3.

My sobriety today may be challenged by:

1.

2.

3.

How can I stay sober today?

1.

2.

3.

Day 7: Old Ways Won't Open New Doors

The first step towards getting somewhere is to decide that you're not going to stay where you are – JP Morgan.

How did you feel when you first picked up this journal and decided you were going to work through it to enjoy a month of sobriety? Excited? Nervous? Hopeful? Dubious?

However you felt is fine.

But did you really take on board that you would have to make some serious changes to your life if you were going to make this work?

The reality is that "old ways won't open new doors". If you're still going to the pub, hanging out with the same drinking mates, and talking about the same things you've always talked about (likely alcohol, maybe followed by drugs), you're almost guaranteed to start drinking alcohol again.

You've set yourself a challenge. It's hard to be alcohol-free when everything seems to be lubricated by alcohol – business deals, relationships, life events... You name it, and someone will find an excuse to drink to it. Then, when you throw in alcohol's known addictive qualities, it's challenging to keep your commitment to yourself to stay sober.

You don't have to become a social recluse for the month, but you will find it helps enormously if you mix things up. Take this as an opportunity to start that evening class or take up that hobby you've been thinking about but haven't started. This will help you meet new people in an alcohol-free setting.

Do a form of exercise that appeals to you – you could join a football or netball team, go to a dance class, try yoga or Pilates, or go for a swim. If you are really bat-shit crazy, try a CrossFit class. Do something you know you'll enjoy to simply have fun without alcohol being part of it. This isn't about losing weight (although you will find that regular exercise will positively impact your body) as it is about changing and replacing old habits with new ones.

If exercise doesn't sound like fun, that's okay. Do whatever works for you. But do something new. Make a change. Nothing changes if nothing changes and you'll go back to the same old same old you're desperately trying to escape.

You're a week into your sobriety (or if you prefer days, 7 days sober), so by now, you might be noticing subtle changes in your behaviour. You have consciously been trying to change your habits and behaviours around alcohol with the sole intention of staying sober. You are taking positive action towards where you want to be in life, which is incredibly powerful.

You are actively creating a positive feedback loop that will have your intuition firing on autopilot, resulting in long-lasting positive changes for your physical, mental, emotional, spiritual, and financial health.

When you see the difference between a positive feedback loop and a negative feedback loop, it makes it easier to see why so many people in positive feedback loops are getting ahead in life.

A positive feedback loop (New ways):

Go to the gym > eat nutritious food > get an early night > wake up fresh > give 100% at work > go to a sound healing session

A negative feedback loop (Old ways):

Go to the pub > get a beer and burger meal > drink all night > pick up drugs > go clubbing > get a takeaway > do more drugs > get no sleep > try not to get sacked > get another takeaway > fall asleep on the sofa

The difference between how you feel internally and externally is a world apart. When you compound the negative feedback loop, week after week, month after month and year after year, it's hardly surprising that people (like myself) end up in rehab.

The people who are winning at life practice the positive feedback loop daily! While you might think in your early days that those activities are boring, the reality is that it's more boring living the rest of your life being hungover and unhappy.

You might not be seeing the results mentioned in '*Giving Up Alcohol*' after seven days, but you will start seeing them over this Challenge, so keep going!

Question for the day – You have to do something different to get something different – what are you doing differently to stay sober? Write a list of what you are doing differently to achieve your new goal of sobriety and how that is helping towards that goal.

If your list is lacking, think of more things you can add to it that will help you stay sober – maybe go to your first AA and/or SMART recovery meeting, find a local therapist you can book eight sessions in to unravel why you feel like this or do your first post into the Sober On A Drunk Planet community to say Hi.

Top tip: The hardest one you list is likely to be the one that will give you the most growth in your sobriety and life, so don't be afraid to jump into the deep end.

Journal Space To Write

Journal Space To Write

Evening Journal

This evening I feel:

What could you have done better today?

Did you feel triggered to drink today? If so, what triggered you to think about drinking?

What did you do well today to maintain your sobriety?

Day 8

Morning Journal

Today I feel:

I am grateful for:

1.

2.

3.

My sobriety today may be challenged by:

1.

2.

3.

How can I stay sober today?

1.

2.

3.

Day 8: The Friends Who Mind Don't Matter And The Friends Who Matter Don't Mind

I used to walk into a room full of people and wonder if they liked me... now I look around and wonder if I like them – Rikki Gale.

If you're a regular drinker, you've probably developed a group of drinking buddies. Now's the time to ask yourself what you have in common with your friends outside of the drink (and possibly drugs). When you take a long, hard look at your alcohol-fuelled friendships, you may well find that the only thing you share is a love of drink.

If that's the case, you might worry about what you're going to do now you're not drinking and need to take some time out.

Be prepared for a couple of things to happen:

- First, some of your drinking friends might turn their backs on you or belittle your efforts. They're doing you a favour. At this stage in the process, you won't want to be around hard drinkers anyway.

- Next, as your confidence and self-esteem improve as a result of sobriety, you start being pickier about who you choose to spend your precious time with. Remember what we said about becoming a Sober Jedi?

You are the average of the five people you spend most of your time with. If those five people like getting drunk, it's no surprise you are here. As you step into your new sober identity, you'll want to take a long hard look at who you're spending your time with. What kind of person do you aspire to be? Who do you know who represents that?

If you don't know anyone, it's time to find new friends.

These 31 days are a form of self-care for YOU. It's not selfish to want to look after yourself. It's essential. If someone else has a problem with you wanting to be your best self, that's their problem, not yours.

You will find that some people will remove themselves from your social circle. Watch out for those who ask, "can't you just come out for one?" or say things like "one drink won't make any difference" or "you used to be *fun!*" You don't need to spend time with them, at least not at this stage when sobriety is still new. You need people who want to support your choices, not belittle them. Have you considered that your choice to ditch your bad habits makes them uncomfortable about their choices?

Again, that's their problem, not yours.

When you're sober, you become confident in saying "no". If you can say no to the drink and drugs, then saying no to other life events becomes a lot easier.

Lean into the JOMO (Joy of Missing Out). When you say no to spending the night in the pub, you have all the time to do something you want to do. You'll also have the money to do it, the energy to do it and the ambition to create an even better life for yourself.

Question of the day – What activities do you do with the five people you spend most of the time with?

Top tip: Be vigilant about people's reactions to your sobriety journey because it says a lot about them and their own drinking/drugging behaviours. Also, be mindful of those who keep wanting to drag you back into drinking – they will want to find someone to justify their own drinking with (Monday night drinks anyone?!).

Stay in your lane, and don't be swayed by people's opinions of your sobriety. This is YOUR journey.

Journal Space To Write

Journal Space To Write

Evening Journal

This evening I feel:

What could you have done better today?

Did you feel triggered to drink today? If so, what triggered you to think about drinking?

What did you do well today to maintain your sobriety?

Day 9

Morning Journal

Today I feel:

I am grateful for:

1.

2.

3.

My sobriety today may be challenged by:

1.

2.

3.

How can I stay sober today?

1.

2.

3.

Day 9: An Attitude Of Gratitude Can Save Your Life

When life is sweet, say thank you and celebrate. When life is bitter, say thank you and grow – Shauna Niequist.

If you've been journaling daily, you'll have nine days of gratitude under your belt. You may not realise it yet, but gratitude is an integral part of getting and staying sober.

Why?

Society programs us to always want more. We feel that we need to keep up with the Joneses and exceed them. The neighbours build an extension, we have to build a bigger one. They get a new car, we have to get a more expensive one.

Yet no matter how much we acquire, how much we 'beat' our neighbours, it's never enough. We don't get a deep, lasting sense of fulfilment.

So we keep striving for more, kidding ourselves that we'll eventually be happy and content. No wonder so many of us use alcohol to 'help' us cope with this sense of failure despite all the trappings of success.

It's a vicious cycle. You're miserable because you don't have the millions in the bank you want, so you turn to a drug that makes it almost impossible to live up to your potential. So you become even more miserable and start resenting your life and everything about it.

When I was working in finance, I was always focused on what was around the corner. The next bonus, the next pay rise, the next promotion. Nothing was good enough. Nothing made me happy.

It's crazy when I look back now. I had a home, a well-paying job and loving family and friends, but I didn't appreciate any of it. I just looked at those around me and envied them for having the things I didn't.

Had I known that gratitude was the secret sauce to happiness, maybe I wouldn't have felt the need to numb the pain of not having everything I wanted with booze and drugs.

Gratitude makes me feel fulfilled in a way alcohol never did. It's free, and it keeps away feelings of envy, dissatisfaction and entitlement, which were old triggering emotions for me to drink, and they might be for you as well.

Twelve-step programs incorporate gratitude because it works. Some of the worst drunks and addicts have used gratitude to transform their lives and get sober for good. If you want to follow them, you need to start being grateful for everything you have.

Gratitude has been an integral part of my sobriety. It helps me stay grounded and humble. It gives me perspective so that when I start to chase after 'more', I can see it for what it is and keep my ego in check.

When you start being grateful for what you've already got, what you don't have loses its importance and has less of an emotional hold over you. That is huge! It helps you resist the urge to hit the old fuck it button when you're having a bad day so you don't pick up that drink.

As you write out the three things you're grateful for each morning, take a moment to allow yourself to really lean into that emotion. Let it fill your whole being so that you can't help smiling because you've got it so *good*.

Here are a few things you can include in your daily gratitude practice if you're stuck for inspiration:

- I'm grateful for waking up sober.
- I'm grateful I woke up with a clear head.
- I'm grateful for a good night's sleep.
- I'm grateful the sun is shining.
- I'm grateful for the rain to water my plants.
- I'm grateful my children are in good health.
- I'm grateful for the Sober On A Drunk Planet Podcast, Online Community and having the space to feel heard.

What do you notice about this list (apart from the fact I am shamelessly plugging the brand again)?

There isn't a single material item on it. I didn't include "I'm grateful for my sportscar" or "I'm grateful for my end-of-year bonus". These are superficial things, and when you practice gratitude, you'll soon discover that material things don't hold as much value as the important things in life.

The list also included gratitude for things outside of yourself. If you remember what we covered about vibrations and energy, energy grows where your attention goes. The more you look for things in your life to be grateful for, the more things life gives you to be grateful for.

It's also helpful to dive deep into why you feel grateful for something. You could say, "I'm grateful for my dog", but take a moment to think about what your dog does for you to make you feel that way. Maybe it's that he makes you feel safe and secure, or he gives you comfort when you're feeling down, or simply that his cute face makes you smile when you come home at the end of the day. Or you are grateful that they have taught you about unconditional love as you clean up the big poop they just did on the carpet (again).

As with all the practices in this journal, consistency is key. Gratitude helps you replace the negative spiral of alcohol with a positive feedback loop that strengthens the more you practice it.

And it works! Millions of sober people around the world can attest to its power.

My own experience with gratitude, and from what I have seen with countless others, is summed beautifully by this quote:

"Wear gratitude like a cloak and it will feed every corner of your life" – Rumi.

Rumi was really onto something even back in 1207.

Question for the day – Yes, we have done lots of gratitude, but it's a practice you can never do too much of!

What are you grateful for at this moment? Have a think before writing it down, and go as deep with those thoughts as you can.

Remember that a deep sense of gratitude harbours stronger positive emotions, so the deeper you go, the better.

Journal Space To Write

Journal Space To Write

Evening Journal

This evening I feel:

What could you have done better today?

Did you feel triggered to drink today? If so, what triggered you to think about drinking?

What did you do well today to maintain your sobriety?

Day 10

Morning Journal

Today I feel:

I am grateful for:

1.

2.

3.

My sobriety today may be challenged by:

1.

2.

3.

How can I stay sober today?

1.

2.

3.

Day 10: Contemplating Your First Sober Night Out And How To Approach It

I chose sober because I wanted a better life. I stay sober because I got one – Anon.

Now that you're over a week into your sobriety journey, you might be starting to think about going out again. Although there's no pressure – if you don't feel ready, that's absolutely fine. Do what works for you, and don't worry about anyone else.

How do you enjoy a night out alcohol-free when your social life used to heavily rely on alcohol?

Here are three tips to support you on your first alcohol-free night out:

1. **Plan ahead.** Consider all the potential scenarios that might come up and then devise a strategy for dealing with them. You might like to recruit a friend or a fellow non-drinker to support you. You could volunteer to be the designated driver. Many venues now have a wide range of alcohol-free wines and beers, so you can view the drinks menu in advance to see what alcohol-free drink you will

have - avoiding the awkward pause, contemplate and potentially cave-in scenario.

2. **Have an exit strategy (and remember the Big Red Fuck It Button Version 2.0).** You might find that it's simply too much, and you're not quite ready to deal with avoiding alcohol on a night out. That's okay. Figure out in advance what you're going to do when it's time to leave, no matter how early or late that might be. And remember, at any point, you can always push the newly upgraded "Big Red Fuck It" button so you can go home, protect your sobriety and inner peace (which are priceless!).

3. **Don't go.** You might find that even thinking about going out brings you out in cold sweats. If going out is causing you more stress than it's worth, the simplest solution is to stay home. For three months after leaving rehab, I stayed in for the evenings or went to AA meetings/group therapy, went to bed early and listened to thousands of hours of audiobooks. That worked for me because alcohol/drugs were such a big part of my life I needed that time to disconnect the power of all my triggers (which seemed like everything). Only you

will know what you feel comfortable with, so go with your gut.

There's no shame in deciding that a situation isn't right for you at the moment. Put yourself first and move at your own pace. Remember JOMO. You'll know when the time is right for you to go out, so don't try to force things before you're ready. Otherwise, you'll end up undermining all your hard work.

If in doubt, don't go out – you are trying to stay sober, so anything that feels like that might be compromised, you have ultimate control of what you do.

Question for the day – What are your biggest challenges to staying sober if you went on a night out? Write a list of obstacles you might expect if you were to go on a night out (you might have already witnessed some).

Visualising obstacles before they happen gives that scenario less power if they materialise. It's like going to your local pub and expecting everyone before you arrive to ask you, "why are you not drinking?" and if some of them do ask that in real-time, you are less phased by it and are armed with a response (try Sienna Green's book, 101 Ways To Say I Quit Drinking for some witty inspiration).

It might be that you actually want a life away from the pub/bars, and you want a new life that doesn't involve late nights, cueing at the bar for ages before getting served, talking bollocks and not hearing anyone because the music is so loud.

You will be surprised by what you no longer tolerate when you get sober!

Journal Space To Write

Journal Space To Write

Evening Journal

This evening I feel:

What could you have done better today?

Did you feel triggered to drink today? If so, what triggered you to think about drinking?

What did you do well today to maintain your sobriety?

Day 11

Morning Journal

Today I feel:

I am grateful for:

1.

2.

3.

My sobriety today may be challenged by:

1.

2.

3.

How can I stay sober today?

1.

2.

3.

Day 11: Individual Therapy

Pain in this life is not avoidable, but the pain we create avoiding pain is avoidable – RD Laing.

While group therapy is great and highly effective, it's not for everyone. If you don't feel comfortable going to a group, can't find an accessible group in your area or simply don't want to go, you may prefer to find a therapist who provides one-to-one support. While group counselling offers an environment where everyone helps each other by sharing experiences and tools they've found effective, you might find that having private therapy enables you to dig deeper into your personal circumstances and drill down into the root cause of your drinking.

If therapy is going to work, you need to find a therapist who is a good fit for you. You develop a very personal relationship with your therapist, and you've got to feel secure enough to open up otherwise you're wasting both your time and money.

Trust allows a therapist to ask searching questions that will challenge you, and yes, that can sometimes be really awkward, and your ego might feel attacked. But if we are not challenging the way we think, we will stay in the same old mindset that got us drunk in the first place. Self-growth requires you to be challenged, and well-trained therapists do that best.

The best way I can explain drinking and the need to get therapy is this:

Drinking is the band-aid/plaster used to mask the initial wound. Something that happened to you in the past is what caused that initial wound, and no matter how much you try to cover that wound up with drink and drugs, the pain will always come through if the initial wound is left untreated. You need to look deep below the surface to truly understand what's going on and to be able to properly heal. Only when you properly heal can you remove the band-aid (drink).

Therapists are trained to help you discover why that wound happened in the first place and help you heal from it. That wound can be past trauma and/or a flawed way of thinking that has impacted you. It could be something you might see as irrelevant as an adult that was said to you as a child, and you have carried that flawed thinking with you into adult life, e.g. I am not good enough, I am a burden, I am fat and ugly. Alcohol and drugs might be the only thing that has temporarily stopped those feelings from re-surfacing, but no matter how much you drink, they always come back, and the negative feedback loop starts again.

If you decide you'd like to try therapy (and I will bang on about how life-changing individual therapy is for the rest of my life), here are some tips for finding the right therapist:

- Don't just go for the first person you come across, even if they come highly recommended by someone you know. Take the time to interview at least two or three before you decide who to work with. There may not be a 'click' between you, which is no reflection on either of you. Sometimes the chemistry isn't there, and that's just how it is. Listen to your instincts about who will be a good fit for you.
- If you can, go for a therapist who has a few years of professional experience under their belt. Ideally, you want someone with as much experience as possible, but be aware that this will likely be reflected in their fee. Find a balance between what you can afford and the best option.

- Whilst you might like to work with someone who feels like a good friend, a good therapist will maintain boundaries and not go into details about their personal life because it can impact the therapeutic relationship. Find someone who will be good at challenging you and isn't afraid to ask the tough questions you have been shying away from.
- Choose someone you feel you can trust. Without that trust, you won't be able to open up to them; without that vulnerability, you won't be able to go deep enough for effective healing.
- Make sure your therapist has the appropriate qualifications. Qualifying as an accredited therapist takes years, including hours of supervised sessions.

You can find a list of accredited therapists in the UK at www.bacp.co.uk. If you're in the United States, you can find a psychologist at www.psychologytoday.com/us/therapists or www.findapsychologist.org. Wherever you are in the world, your doctor or Private Healthcare provider might be able to provide further details of suitable local therapists.

If you can find a therapist you like and trust, you'll discover that they'll help you take giant leaps down the road to recovery. It should be one of the most challenging yet rewarding relationships you have in your lifetime.

If you have a severe problem with alcohol/drugs and you can't manage a few days without it – you need as much help as possible (I have the t-shirt of self-denial and spiralled for two years before getting the appropriate level of care). The strongest approach to recovery is a mixture of individual therapy (which might come as part of a rehab programme/doctor referral or private referral), AA/SMART group meetings, joining online communities and other sober/recovery groups. Yes, you can pick a few of these at a time, but ultimately the above mix is where we see the best results for long-term sobriety.

Therapy is my go-to when things in sobriety are feeling tough. Having the self-awareness now, I can put my ego aside and go to therapy to work through situations in my life (not just sobriety-related) that I am struggling with. The results are instant, and the feeling that a weight has been lifted never tires. Therapy helps, no matter how sober you are!

Top tip: A great therapist/counsellor will help you find the answers within yourself; they won't tell you what to do. If you can afford it, pay for therapists/counsellors with lots of experience, as they will help you get to the answers quicker.

(And if you think, "I don't need therapy" – try four sessions before making that conclusion – everyone in the world is carrying something that is unhealthy)

Question for the day – Why did you drink to the point of unhappiness? Think about what might be lacking in your life that you had to use alcohol/drugs to silence that unhappiness. Have a good think before writing anything down.

Journal Space To Write

Journal Space To Write

Evening Journal

This evening I feel:

What could you have done better today?

Did you feel triggered to drink today? If so, what triggered you to think about drinking?

What did you do well today to maintain your sobriety?

Day 12

Morning Journal

Today I feel:

I am grateful for:

1.

2.

3.

My sobriety today may be challenged by:

1.

2.

3.

How can I stay sober today?

1.

2.

3.

Day 12: Death of the Ego

Don't let your new sober ego get the better of you – Sean Alexander.

(Yes, I just quoted myself – Ego anyone?)

Your ego isn't inherently bad. It's actually a very important part of our self, the aspect which tries to keep you safe. Believe it or not, it has your best interests at heart – it just has some funny ways of showing it at times.

Your ego develops from childhood. Your experiences of the world around you gave rise to thoughts that created beliefs that turned into behaviours.

But your ego can also develop some strange ideas that distort our interpretation of reality, making us act as who we think we are rather than our true selves. It's what keeps us in our comfort zone, even if that comfort zone is booze-soaked and not that comfortable. To the ego, safe is more important than happy – or sober.

Alcohol and drugs are disastrous for the ego. It can be an uncontrollable beast at the best of times without adding addictive substances into the mix. Drink can give rise to an alter ego – we can be a totally different person when we've had a few. If you have ever watched the film "Old School" and seen the character "Frank The Tank" – that was my ego under the influence of alcohol and drugs. But when I was sober, I would be shy and introverted (my true character, which I now love).

You can spot an over-inflated ego a mile off. Complaining about other people and blaming them for all your troubles is one sign – and I bet you hear that a lot at the pub. Others include arrogance, clinging to grudges, resenting those around you, refusing to admit fault, talking over others, and taking credit for other people's achievements.

Our ego makes us think we're more important than we really are. We see ourselves as better than those around us, like we have nothing more to learn.

But you and I both know there's *always* more to learn. That's why you're working through this Challenge.

A simple test to see how out of control your ego is, is to note your reaction the next time you receive criticism or feedback. Do you have nothing to learn from the critique or feedback, or is your ego refusing to hear and jumping to defend itself?

Your ego can get in the way of your sobriety. This is why you might have tried to quit drinking in the past, managed a few weeks, months, or years, and then relapsed. Your ego thought the job was done when really you were only getting started. It wanted to return to your comfort zone where you could drink whatever you wanted whenever you wanted because that was familiar.

Here are a few ways you can get control of your ego:

- **Be vigilant.** Start becoming a conscious observer of what you say when talking about yourself. Are you inflating the truth about your actual reality to impress others? When people ask you what you do for a living, do you tell them the truth or inflate it to match what you think will impress them more? Be conscious of statements that you start with 'I', 'me', 'my' and 'myself' as they could be driven by your ego. Try active listening over letting your ego respond straight away – let the other person's words soak in before coming back with a response (anything that's instant can be driven by the ego again).
- **Stay humble.** Whether it's helping someone just because you can, practising gratitude, journaling

your thoughts or actively listening, look for ways to keep yourself grounded. Acknowledge your flaws and own them when you make a mistake.

- **Be teachable.** Your ego will trick you into thinking that you know it already. If you did, then you wouldn't have the problems you do. Be open to getting help from others and accept there will be people who know more than you do – and that's okay. You can learn from them. Always try to be the student and never the master.

- **Stay out of ego battles.** We've already talked about how keeping up with the Joneses causes all sorts of problems. So don't even try. If you find yourself getting sucked into competitions over who has the biggest house or makes the most money, step back and don't engage.

- **Don't talk – do**. You don't need to tell people about your achievements. They speak for themselves. Even better, do things for the sheer joy of doing them and don't worry about whether they'll impress anyone.

- **Stop chasing likes**. Social media is designed to flatter the ego with the dopamine rush from getting plenty of "likes". Take care you don't get caught up in chasing attention in the form of positive feedback – it's just another form of addiction.

- **Stick to the facts**. The ego hates to admit it's wrong. Don't get drawn into debates that go nowhere. Google for the correct answer, learn something if needed, and move on. And yes, we all know someone who still doesn't admit they're wrong even after googling the answer.

The more you understand your ego and how it functions, the more self-aware you'll become. You'll be open to learning and staying grounded, which will help you stay sober, even when it's tough.

Sobriety delivers a million benefits, something you will witness over time, but if unmanaged, these benefits can feed the ego, and you start to become complacent around your drinking – your ego thinks you are stronger than an addictive and poisonous substance. The reality is that you have never been part of the "one and done club" and a common theme for relapse is that people "think they would be alright". The harsh truth is they never do just have one drink and go back to square one or go even further backwards. Your drinking past will tell you what your drinking future is like, so don't let your ego tell you otherwise. Never get complacent because alcohol will always be an addictive substance.

Question for the day – Think about a recent time (and for future situations) where you have bitched and moaned about other people – ask yourself this – what is really going on for you that you have to bitch and/or moan about others?

Write down any thoughts below.

You can use the emotions wheel to identify the emotion that you think your ego might be trying to protect you from. For example, I was bitching about Wendy in the office today because she made me feel threatened (fear) because the boss promoted her and not me. That fear opened up a can of insecurities that my ego was trying to protect me from, like not being good enough.

Journal Space To Write

Journal Space To Write

Evening Journal

This evening I feel:

What could you have done better today?

Did you feel triggered to drink today? If so, what triggered you to think about drinking?

What did you do well today to maintain your sobriety?

Day 13

Morning Journal

Today I feel:

I am grateful for:

1.

2.

3.

My sobriety today may be challenged by:

1.

2.

3.

How can I stay sober today?

1.

2.

3.

Day 13: The Hardest Lift Of All – Getting Your Butt Off The Couch

Strong body (and gut) = strong mind.

We all know that exercise is essential for a healthy body and mind, but society puts pressure on us that makes exercise seem downright depressing. You've probably seen countless ads telling you to lose weight and gain muscle. Eating healthy food and exercising regularly will make you look fabulous, and admirers will flock to you.

Can you say ego? And you know the problems with ego!

If we take our appearance out of the equation and look at the other benefits of exercise, it becomes clear that there are countless reasons to exercise that have nothing to do with our ego and everything to do with our health.

Your drinking may have been a significant factor in your not exercising. The last thing you feel like doing is lifting heavy weights or taking part in a spin class when you're hungover, and given the choice between exercise or the pub after work, the pub's the easy option.

But when you choose alcohol over exercise, you kickstart the negative feedback loop of lethargy > lack of motivation

> depression > leading you right back to the pub. Over time, this negative feedback loop is BAD news for every area of your life. Your health is your wealth – without it, we are speeding up the ticking time bomb known as death.

One of the reasons why I became a personal trainer was because I witnessed first-hand the impact exercise had on my sobriety. One of the most rewarding things for me was going to an exercise class or hitting the gym for an hour or so.

Getting fit also helped me to undo the damage caused by years of abusing my body. Some of the benefits included:

- More energy. The type where you can skip into work on a Monday and high-five everyone (yes, you can also be "that person" everyone hates because they are upbeat and full of energy).
- Improved insulin sensitivity (which helps reduce sugar cravings, which often hit when you first go sober).
- Improved mood and lower stress due to the release of endorphins. These same endorphins help fuel the positive feedback loop and give you a natural high without the hangover.

- Emotional regulation helps massively with sobriety. Probably one of the most understated reasons to get into fitness because emotional regulation is massive for living a sober life with all its benefits.

- Improved liver and kidney function thanks to more blood pumping around the body, as well as eliminating more toxins.

- Helps combat fatty liver disease.

- A natural confidence because you look and feel better. This confidence also helps you resist alcohol because you feel more at ease in social situations. You are also armed with ego tools so that you can go and get your chiselled abs and peachy bum and NOT turn into an egomaniac in the process (we all know somebody like that).

- Improved cognitive function and problem-solving skills. A clear head helps you make better choices, and I can't underestimate how much clearer life becomes. Sober extremists term this new state of consciousness as "radical clarity", and they are right.

- Undoes the damage caused by the sedentary lifestyle associated with drinking. Alcoholics predominantly have flat bums because of all the sitting down they do, and sobriety will allow you the ability to work on building the "bowling ball butt" if that's what you want.

- Replaces drunk goals with sober fitness goals. Setting fitness goals can be done using the SMART framework, giving you more motivation if there is an end goal to your training.

- Improved quality of sleep. When you only sleep for four out of seven nights when in active addiction versus eight hours every night in sobriety – it's a lifesaver for your mental and physical health.

- Because of all the benefits mentioned above – I can work longer, smarter and have a thirst for learning, which has enabled me to earn more money and LOVE what I do. Without exercising and using it to help regulate emotions in sobriety, I wouldn't have achieved half the things I have today (including this book series).

- Lowers risk for a range of conditions, including coronary heart disease, stroke, type 2 diabetes, bowel cancer, breast cancer, early death, osteoarthritis, depression and dementia.

Honestly? That's just the tip of the iceberg. I could write an entire book about the benefits of exercise. Movement is medicine, and it goes way beyond the superficial goals of losing weight and gaining muscle.

With so many options, there's no excuse to start exercising. Do whatever appeals to you – go to the gym, sign up for a class, take a walk, join a sports team, download an exercise app or follow some yoga videos on YouTube. Do *anything* as long as it gets your heart and lungs pumping.

If your finances allow, you might like to hire a personal trainer or strength and conditioning coach to give you accountability. They'll help you set realistic goals and help you reach them. A more economical alternative is to attend a group-based session and get accountability from fellow group members.

There's nothing like the natural high you get from exercise. I have yet to take a client through a personal training session and not have them say how great they feel afterwards. It's a much better feeling than the highs you get from alcohol that soon come crashing down into a low.

They say the "hardest lift of all is lifting your butt off the couch", and alcohol can make that lift even harder. But just as no one feels worse for getting sober, no one regrets exercising – unless they were exercising through a hangover!

Exercise is a fantastic way of establishing that all-important positive feedback loop that helps you stay sober. It does come with a warning though – exercise can help you become incredibly fit, happy, and enable you to fit into those trousers you never thought you could!

Exercising is brilliant but it doesn't complete the full holistic approach that Sober On A Drunk Planet promotes.

We have your gut health to consider as well. How often have you thought about all the substances you put into your body and how they react with your gut?

Alcohol is literally the WORST thing you can pour into your stomach (which is part of the gut) because it is a poison. If alcohol was invented today, it wouldn't be sold for consumption because of what it does to people.

If you just imagine hand sanitisers that are primarily alcohol-based. They use alcohol because it is proven to kill off bacteria on your hands. Imagine what it does to your body's gut bacteria when you down that pint or finish that bottle of wine off? Developing a gut microbiome (a home for gut bacteria to grow) with the right balance of bacteria in our gut is one of the most important things we must look after for our overall health!

Having excellent gut health also feeds the intuition we talk about in the 3 sober steps because we need a well-nourished gut to help make those all-important decisions on autopilot that will keep us in a healthy feedback loop.

Removing alcohol from your gut is a MASSIVE bonus for your overall health because:

- Alcohol causes various types of cancer and the contents are processed via the gut (it's not a maybe or a possible; it's a FACT),
- Skin conditions and other illnesses can be caused by an inflammatory response from your gut, which alcohol can contribute heavily towards.
- Acid reflux, leaky gut and other gross-sounding conditions are heavily linked to alcohol use. You might even suffer from some of them.
- Your gut is your second brain - You have more nerves going from your stomach to your brain than the other way around – nature is sending us a clear message to look after our guts! The vagus nerve is central to our mental well-being and is negatively

impacted when we have poor gut health – Adding alcohol into the mix doesn't help!

So it's not just a case of understanding how to lift weights in the gym or survive your first CrossFit class; it's about fuelling yourself with nutritious foods that will help bolster your physical and mental strength, contributing to your staying sober.

Don't beat yourself up if you are eating more food than usual during this Challenge (we have all been there) – focus on staying sober.

Just like people, places, and things can impact your energy levels, so does food. Start to become aware of those foods that help and those that hinder.

Questions for the day – How are you progressing in your health and fitness (exercise and eating healthy)?

What would you like to try?

What is holding you back from starting?

Whatever your excuses are for not starting to do some form of exercise (walking is exercise) they are known as your "limiting beliefs" – you can exercise, you just choose to put barriers in place. Don't be a prisoner in your own head; just sign up for something and get going – I promise you won't regret it.

Journal Space To Write

Journal Space To Write

Evening Journal

This evening I feel:

What could you have done better today?

Did you feel triggered to drink today? If so, what triggered you to think about drinking?

What did you do well today to maintain your sobriety?

Day 14

Morning Journal

Today I feel:

I am grateful for:

1.

2.

3.

My sobriety today may be challenged by:

1.

2.

3.

How can I stay sober today?

1.

2.

3.

Day 14: Let Go Of The Past

Resentment is like drinking poison and waiting for the other person to die - Malachy McCourt.

Now is a good time to turn our attention to resentments. It plays a pivotal role in twelve-step programs, turning bitter, angry alcoholics into content, forgiving, compassionate, sober people.

Whether AA's approach resonates with you or not, there's no doubt it's worked for many people over the decades. Dealing with resentment is crucial to its success.

Being resentful has two significant negative effects:

1. It prevents you from being present in the moment because your focus is on events in the past that made you resentful, such as being passed over for promotion because the boss favoured someone else for the role.
2. Resentment requires a lot of energy. You have to think about what's annoyed you all the time to stay resentful, constantly bringing up the trigger incident in your mind, which also carries the risk of continued physical stress from something that happened weeks, months or even years ago.

When you can deal with resentment, you can be entirely in the moment in your everyday life. You're also conserving your energy for those things that truly matter rather than pouring it into the past or things you can't control.

If you're filled with resentment, it takes time to learn how to let it go. But as you start to recognise that it doesn't serve you to bear grudges, it becomes easier to let them go. A grudge keeps you in the cycles of negativity that have trapped you in alcohol's control.

By the time I was finally ready to quit drinking, I hated everyone around me. They were all doing so much better than me, and I resented them for it. I came off social media because all I could see were people doing well, and I couldn't bear that they were happy and I wasn't. It only made me feel worse about myself.

My resentment really came from the fact I was so incredibly unhappy with myself and my life. Alcohol and drugs had given me temporary relief, and it seemed the only way out. Thank goodness I made the decision to go to rehab, or that resentment might have devoured me alive.

It was a vicious cycle – I believed I was worthless, so I behaved in ways that made me worthless. Resentment sent me straight to the bottle.

It was tough to break this cycle until I got serious about getting sober and reached step four of the twelve-step program – releasing resentment.

Resentment is a powerful emotion that has seen many people in sobriety turn back to alcohol because it's the only solution they found to relieve how bad resentment was making them feel. This is why understanding our resentments and confronting them is such an essential part of long-term sobriety.

When you start writing out a list of who and what you resent, it becomes easy to identify the underlying pattern: alcohol makes you think it's you against the world! Who would want to live a life filled with hate for everyone and everything? Yet, this is what alcohol does to us – and you can probably see this pattern in people you know who complain all the time.

At the end of today's reflection, we have included a resentments table, which is labelled as follows:

1. Who/what do I resent?
2. What caused my resentment?
3. What emotion does this make me feel? (Refer to the Wheel of Emotion for help with this)
4. What do I achieve by letting this resentment go?

Now fill in each column with as much detail as possible. Take as much time as you need – it takes some people in AA years to complete this step because they've allowed so many resentments to build up. But as you work through it, you soon feel its therapeutic effect, especially if your baggage has accrued over the years.

So, for example, in the first column, you might list your colleague, Wendy. You resent her because she got a bigger bonus than you. This made you feel unvalued and depressed. By letting go of this resentment, you can ask for feedback on why you didn't get a bigger bonus and start finding ways to improve your performance so you can get a bigger bonus next time.

You can return to this exercise as much as you like, even after you get sober. Even though I've stopped drinking, I sometimes find myself feeling resentful of others. The difference now is that when it arises, I can see it for what it is, process it and release it. I find that when I resent others, it's often a reflection of how I'm feeling, such as angry, scared, sad or left out, rather than because they've done something to provoke me. Indeed, most of the time, the person you're resenting doesn't have a clue you've spent all this time and energy resenting them!

Letting go of resentments is a huge step towards being free from those things you can't control like people, situations, or things and replaces it with control over one of the most potent emotions behind relapses. When you can control resentment without needing to drink, it's incredibly liberating.

When you can spot resentment when it arises and understand its effect on you, you can work to alleviate its influence so you can stay sober. With time, you'll find you feel it less and less, and when you do, you know exactly how to kick it into touch – without a drink.

Resentments Table

(If you are as bitter as I was by the end of my drinking, you might need to get an extra writing pad!)

Who/what do I resent?	What caused my resentment?	What emotion does this make me feel?	What do I achieve by letting this resentment go?
Wendy	*Receiving a higher bonus than me*	*Fearful that I am not good enough*	*Losing energy to something I can't control and to look at my own performance to see where I can improve*

Who/what do I resent?	What caused my resentment?	What emotion does this make me feel?	What do I achieve by letting this resentment go?

Who/what do I resent?	What caused my resentment?	What emotion does this make me feel?	What do I achieve by letting this resentment go?

This list can get quite long, so if you run out of space, use the additional table in the Appendix.

Evening Journal

This evening I feel:

What could you have done better today?

Did you feel triggered to drink today? If so, what triggered you to think about drinking?

What did you do well today to maintain your sobriety?

Day 15
Morning Journal

Today I feel:

I am grateful for:

1.

2.

3.

My sobriety today may be challenged by:

1.

2.

3.

How can I stay sober today?

1.

2.

3.

Day 15: The Sober Awakening

And just like that, it all made sense – A Sober Extremist talking about radical clarity.

One of the reasons why no one can predict what their sober journey will look like is because there are so many unexpected benefits, but they are different for everyone.

Many people drink to numb their emotions, so when they stop drinking, they have to face something they've been avoiding for a long time – years, decades even. This can be tough to begin with, but if you can stick with it (perhaps with the help of a trained professional or a support group), you'll find that a lot of the problems you were drinking to escape simply aren't there anymore.

As your body and mind clear themselves of the fog brought on by alcohol, you find alternative solutions to the physical, mental, emotional and spiritual problems you were hiding from with alcohol.

In my case, sobriety allowed me to see that my corporate job had made me soulless (along with the drink and drugs). All those years, I thought I wanted the status – not to mention the pay packet it brought - when the truth was none of it was right for me. Drinking was keeping me trapped in a situation that wasn't serving me. I was never going to find fulfilment in that job, no matter how many people thought I was lucky to be able to enjoy the lifestyle it brought.

It was only by doing the work, which involved individual and group therapy, attending anonymous meetings in my first year of sobriety, getting a sponsor, doing the step work and lots of reading/listening to self-help books, that I had my sober awakening, which also felt very spiritual.

Yes, that's right, I had a spiritual awakening. Up to that point of getting sober, I had been directionless and went from bar to bar each weekend without ever thinking my life through. My life was flashing before my eyes in a predictable and depressing way, and it was only because of sobriety (and doing the work) that I was able to make those changes. It allows you to take a step back, consciously look at what is working for you and what isn't and then have the energy to make positive changes to put you back on track – none of that was possible on a hangover and no money each month!

From learning so much new information whilst sober, I had learned a completely new perspective about life, which was the radical clarity I mentioned earlier. Some say it's like coming out of the matrix, and you see what the world is truly like behind its layers of code that we have all been following mindlessly. But for me, it's why I called this book series "Sober On A Drunk Planet" because of the radical clarity you develop when you stop using the numbing agent (alcohol/drugs) that so many of us are controlled by. Getting sober allowed me to feel like I was in control of my life for the very first time.

Without alcohol controlling me, I was able to find the courage to take a leap of faith and start my own business. For the first time, I felt like my life was aligned with what I was supposed to do (not what I thought I was supposed to do). Don't be fooled; I have had many setbacks in that time, but when you are aligned with your purpose, you see every setback as a learning opportunity to grow, and nothing will get in your way.

How do you get to the Sober Awakening?

Make sobriety a daily habit coupled with doing the work to get to know who you truly are. The energy you get from being healthy and learning about our world through books/audiobooks, coupled with the radical clarity, are massive steps to get you there.

Going sober can see you creating an entirely new life, one that reflects your true values and desires, so I think it only fair to warn you that if you stick with this life, in three months, you really could be leaving your corporate job, taking up yoga in Bali and starting your own sober commune! Or if sobriety really fucks you up, you might become a regular at CrossFit.

Question for the day – What makes your soul sing?

Look at both work and spare time activities. It's essential to look at work because we spend most of our lives working, so it's even more important to try and be happy for that time!

This question is just to get you thinking about your energy levels and to make you think about what fires you up.

Imagine working in a job where you felt as close to 100% energised each day. Then imagine how far that could get you in the future if you worked at max capacity all the time and not the 30% you currently work on while hungover and depressed.

For example, writing books and running the community lighten my soul. Helping others through something I have been through is life-changing for me. I wake up with passion and purpose and LOVE what I do. I have had a million jobs before this one, and my energy levels for this are 100%. All the jobs I had when I was drinking and drugging saw me work at about 30% capacity on a good day - if you've worked in Finance, you can probably relate!

When you have spare time, what activities make you feel alive when not drinking alcohol?

For example, I love playing golf (if that wasn't already clear). I feel at my best when I am playing golf. I am out in nature, playing a sport and socialising with people – all without needing or wanting to drink. It's my therapy that lights up my soul (even the worst days on the golf course are still better than when I used to work in Finance!).

Journal Space To Write

Journal Space To Write

Evening Journal

This evening I feel:

What could you have done better today?

Did you feel triggered to drink today? If so, what triggered you to think about drinking?

What did you do well today to maintain your sobriety?

The Half-Way Stage

At this point, you've completed just over two weeks alcohol-free, and that's an incredible achievement so far.

It wasn't that long ago you might have thought it impossible when everything and everyone in your life reminds you of alcohol!

It's an excellent point in this Challenge to revisit your promise and remind yourself of why you are doing this.

Remember those prizes of more time, energy, money, and more we discussed at the beginning of the Challenge? They are what you need to remind yourself of why you are doing this, and when you have tasted sobriety for long enough, you will wonder why you hadn't become Sober On A Drunk Planet sooner!

Day 16
Morning Journal

Today I feel:

I am grateful for:

1.

2.

3.

My sobriety today may be challenged by:

1.

2.

3.

How can I stay sober today?

1.

2.

3.

Day 16: Positive Action Leads To More Positive Action

Knowledge is only potential power: Knowledge + Positive Action = Power to make positive changes in your life.

Back when I was drinking, I was stuck in a negative loop where negative actions led to even more negative actions. I'd go out for a drink, do something stupid, wake up with hangxiety, have no energy, no money, feel remorse... then go out and do it all over again.

Lather, rinse, repeat.

I never gave myself any time or space to do something productive. Drinking took priority. I would go to the gym for three weeks before a holiday to get in shape for the beach, but then I'd be right back into old habits when I returned. And with the benefit of hindsight, nobody can get in shape within three weeks (unless they are on steroids and in the gym for 6 hours a day).

Once I removed alcohol from the equation, it became easier for one positive action to be followed by another. Without the booze, I'd wake up fresh the next morning, motivated to make the most of the day, maybe by spending time with my family, getting some exercise or starting a new hobby.

The more I saw positive results, the easier it became to stick with my new, healthy habits.

There's no pill you can pop, no magic wand you can wave that will suddenly enable you to make positive choices. The only way to start that positive cycle is by learning about new ways to live and taking action on what you learn – imperfect action is better than doing nothing at all. Success is only defined by your failures; you can't fail at something if you have never tried. Sobriety is the same.

Before you started working through this journal, you probably knew you'd feel better if you quit drinking. You knew that "just one drink" would turn into three, four, and more. But you had it anyway, accepting you were going to feel like crap afterwards (which is a form of self-harm!).

The only way to change that is to take the right positive action based on the new knowledge you have learned, which supports your commitment to sobriety. You have to *do* something: say no to going out for that one drink, go to the gym, find something better to do with your time. As soon as you start doing something differently, your brain will start building new neural pathways that reinforce this new pattern of behaviour. Gradually, avoiding old habits and making healthier ones becomes easier and easier. It's like a rolling stone. It might take a little while to get started, but once it does, it builds momentum until it's rocketing along!

The key thing in this process is consistency. The first time you wake up without that pesky hangover, you can enjoy your day, be more productive than you thought possible, and lay the foundations for that new healthy feedback loop. You'll feel good, so you have the motivation to do it again.

I know, I know. I make it sound easy when I know full well that it can be incredibly hard sometimes. But it gets easier. Over time, your brain becomes rewired to this new way of being until you wonder why you ever did anything differently.

Remember: you only need to be sober "just for today." One day is all you need to get started. You can layer on another day and another after that, but it starts with one day.

Mistakes happen, no matter how positive our intentions are.

But when we slip up, we have a choice: learn and do something different next time or fall back into our old ways and make the same mistakes over and over again. I bet you're bored of that second choice, right? So choose to do something different that aligns with your goal of staying sober.

Use the journal space below to start by drawing up a list of positive actions that will take you closer towards your goal of staying sober. This practice will help you cement ideas that will help you win this Challenge and remain sober. Some ideas to get you started:

- Go home a different route so you avoid the pub and potential triggers.
- Leave group chats and tell your friends you're having a break from nights out for your well-being. (This also means you don't have to deal with any grief for not going out!)
- If you have a drink while doing certain things, such as the after-round drink at the golf club, go home straight after, order a lime and soda (my alcohol-free drink of choice) or go and play another round

of golf! Break the connection and do an activity that doesn't revolve around the people, places and things that trigger you into craving alcohol.

- Tell your family you can't come to a gathering because you're focusing on your mental health. (It can be harder putting boundaries in place with family than with your friends, but it's equally important if you want to stay sober.)

Once you've got your list, you'll probably notice that the items that seem hardest also happen to be the ones that will get you to your goal fastest. If you can, do these ones first. The results will be worth it.

Your goal right now is to stay sober for just one day. If you're confronted with something that's going to undermine your efforts, like your regular Friday night pub crawl, ask yourself:

"Will my actions take me closer or further away from my goal?"

When you take the time to consciously decide what you do, you'll find it easier to take action in support of your goals rather than mindlessly doing what you've always done and getting the same negative result.

Journal Space To Write

Journal Space To Write

Evening Journal

This evening I feel:

What could you have done better today?

Did you feel triggered to drink today? If so, what triggered you to think about drinking?

What did you do well today to maintain your sobriety?

Day 17

Morning Journal

Today I feel:

I am grateful for:

1.

2.

3.

My sobriety today may be challenged by:

1.

2.

3.

How can I stay sober today?

1.

2.

3.

Day 17: Why Don't You Drink Alcohol?

Because I don't want the embarrassment of wetting the bed again, I'm 37 so it's not as acceptable as it once was – Unknown.

If I had a pound for every time someone questioned my choice to NOT drink alcohol, I would be a millionaire by now. People always questioned my choice around cocaine, but NOT once did anyone (apart from my mum - who was always right) question my INSANE behaviour on alcohol.

We really do live on a drunk planet!

The society we live in has its cultural identities tightly intwined with alcohol (and drugs).

If you are English – I don't even need to write down what everyone thinks of our drinking culture but it's not a good national representation that we have globally! You only need to see "brits abroad" to really understand how awful we are as a nation. Yes, I was once part of that problem and apologise to every Greek and Spanish Island I visited between the ages of 16 to 28!

If you are American - you can't drink until you are 21 years old and for anyone who has been to Spring Break, there is a very good reason why you probably have those laws in place (because Spring Break is utter chaos). America is now known for its opioid crisis, seeing a shocking rise in drug related deaths but also the legalisation of cannabis has become widespread. Drugs and Budweiser anyone?

If you are Irish – you have a drinking problem but it's ok because you are Irish and that's how the world portrays you. Guiness anyone?

If you are Scottish – you drink whiskey and it's likely you are or someone very close to you is an alcoholic, but that's ok, because you are Scottish. If you have ever tasted Whiskey and enjoyed the taste of it – you are lying.

For Italians – you either drink wine or you get expelled from the family (said in a mafia style voice).

The Spanish are known for their sangria (a lethal mix of drugs aka various forms of alcohol) which when vomited leaves the whole place in a red colour - very much like someone has been murdered. But you also have "party islands" like Ibiza where doing drugs is illegal but we all know its legal. You can walk into a bar, get some cocaine and pills, go clubbing for five days solid and pray you get through passport control without anyone noticing the size of your pupils.

It's hardly surprising from the short tour around various drinking and drugging countries, we live on a drunk planet where alcohol is highly celebrated. Other drugs are becoming more acceptable and even starting to see more countries legalize more drugs to try and tackle addiction (but also benefit from the tax).

It's hardly surprising that most people are completely blind to what alcohol actually does to them on a physical, mental and spiritual level. Plus, alcohol is the gateway drug to EVERY OTHER drug known to us. Drug dealers hang around bars and pubs for a reason.

So when the next person asks you "why don't you drink alcohol?" don't hate them for it, it's just part of the conditioning that you are trying to break free from.

Top Tip: It's worth noting that you will need replies to people asking, "why don't you drink alcohol?" because it's one of the most common questions we all get asked (no matter how many years sober we are). You should arm yourself with 101 witty replies by getting a copy of Sienna Greens book – Why Don't You Drink Alcohol? 101 Ways To Say I Quit Drinking Without It Being Awkward (Sort Of).

Question for the day – Write down five replies to people when (and it will happen) they ask you "why don't you drink alcohol?".

Most people either say they are driving or on antibiotics when they give up in the early days and don't feel comfortable opening up and that's fine. It's nobody's business other than yours so you can always tell people to go away and mind their own business. If you are female and over 25 years old, it's likely the person assumes you are pregnant – this is how the drunk planet operates.

If someone asks me that question now, I make sure I tell them my life story, about the book series, the community and everything else sobriety related – they never ask again.

Journal Space To Write

Journal Space To Write

Evening Journal

This evening I feel:

What could you have done better today?

Did you feel triggered to drink today? If so, what triggered you to think about drinking?

What did you do well today to maintain your sobriety?

Day 18

Morning Journal

Today I feel:

I am grateful for:

1.

2.

3.

My sobriety today may be challenged by:

1.

2.

3.

How can I stay sober today?

1.

2.

3.

Day 18: The Power Of Group Therapy

Though no one can go back and make a brand-new start, anyone can start from now and make a brand-new ending – Carl Bard.

You are not alone. It might feel like it sometimes, but you are not the only person walking the path to sobriety. It's much easier to stay on course when you surround yourself with others who share your goal.

You might not know anyone who is sober right now because you only have drinking buddies, but I'm going to tell you the perfect place to find sober friends: at AA/SMART groups, sober meet-up groups and online with the rest of us in the Sober On A Drunk Planet Community (plus lots of other online communities you should try).

Alcoholics Anonymous and SMART Recovery are two well-established organisations with a proven track record of supporting individuals to get and stay sober. They offer a welcoming, non-judgmental environment where you can learn more about the various tools available to help you stay sober. What's more, they allow you to make new friends and broaden your horizons in ways you can't imagine.

Alcoholics Anonymous was founded in 1935 and has been successfully helping problem drinkers with their recovery ever since.

You can find details of your nearest meeting at www.alcoholics-anonymous.org.uk if you're in the UK and www.aa.org if you live elsewhere.

My suggestion, if you are really struggling, is to give them a go, even if you don't think you fit the alcoholic/drug addict mould, because the 12-step programme is a spiritual programme. There is nothing like it in the world, and the only way you can experience it is by doing it. It changed my life for the better, as well as millions of other hopeless drunks.

Plus, there is an AA or some other form of anonymous meeting on every street corner. You just need to have a search on their website for a local meeting if you think I am lying! And to make it even easier, they are online, so you can join a meeting in Los Angeles, London, Ireland, Australia, Canada, Turkey, South Africa, or anywhere you fancy listening to inspiring stories of recovery (24 hours a day). The online meetings are also an excellent tool for helping with cravings if you need an immediate dose of recovery to help keep you sober.

Similar style meetings and step work also exist for family members of alcoholics/drug addicts in the form of al-anon (www.al-anonuk.org.uk and www.al-anon.org/). Having family members on board who are doing work to understand and support you during your own changes is only a positive thing.

It's not just AA; it's cocaine anonymous, narcotics anonymous, overeaters anonymous, and the list is ever-growing as we develop new addictive behaviours. Each meeting has its own vibe, so if you don't find a meeting you like, keep trying other meetings because each differs in the group energy it provides. Always look at the similarities and not the differences when going to meetings, as you are there to recover, not pass judgment on others.

If the AA approach doesn't appeal, you may like to check out SMART Recovery instead.

SMART (Self-Management and Recovery Training) is a secular program that supports people with a range of addictions, including drugs, alcohol, smoking, gambling, eating, shopping, and the internet. Sessions are led by trained facilitators who support attendees to learn to help themselves and each other with a combination of CBT (cognitive behaviour therapy) and other tried and tested tools and methods.

SMART utilises a 4-Point program covering:

- Building and maintaining motivation
- Dealing with urges
- Coping with feelings, thoughts and behaviours
- Living a balanced life.

SMART has a strong focus on personal choice, so you're not forced or coerced into doing anything, but you are supported to take responsibility for your actions.

They hold that people choose to behave in a certain way but can also choose to stop. We all have the ability to choose to change whatever we're doing that's unhelpful or harmful.

Since they do not define people by their behaviours, you are not referred to as an addict or alcoholic. It's not a one-size-fits-all approach either – you're given a range of tools, and it's up to you which ones you choose to use.

You can find details of your nearest SMART group at https://smartrecovery.org.uk if you're in the UK and https://www.smartrecovery.org if you're elsewhere.

Two very different approaches, but both are highly effective. Group therapy played a significant role in my recovery, and it could be the regular meet-up you need to fill those hours with sobriety rather than thinking about drinking.

Task for the day – just find out where your local SMART and AA (or other anonymous meeting if it meets your needs better) meetings are.

These organisations are FREE, and they collectively provide the best recovery programmes the world has seen. If in doubt, just go – you have nothing to lose and everything to gain from them.

Evening Journal

This evening I feel:

What could you have done better today?

Did you feel triggered to drink today? If so, what triggered you to think about drinking?

What did you do well today to maintain your sobriety?

Day 19

Morning Journal

Today I feel:

I am grateful for:

1.

2.

3.

My sobriety today may be challenged by:

1.

2.

3.

How can I stay sober today?

1.

2.

3.

Day 19: Friendships, Sober Dating And Sobering Relationships

Want to find out who your true friends are? Get sober –
Anon.

When you've been wearing beer goggles for years, the world looks very different when you take them off. When your judgement isn't clouded by alcohol, you make very different decisions. You can follow your own instincts instead of going along with whatever seems hilarious at the time, only to wake up later and discover that it was a *really* bad idea. Especially if you ended up being the entertainment (again).

You are a very different person drunk to when you're sober. This means that your relationships will be very different when you take alcohol out of the equation. Some will get a lot better. But others will get worse – or even end completely. And that's fine – it's part of life. People grow older, and they grow in different directions – you are not obliged to be friends or spend time with family that makes you unhappy or makes you feel less about yourself. And remember those "Energy Vampires" we discussed previously; stay away from them at all costs. Life is too short to be constantly drained by other people and their problems; it's hard enough trying to figure it out for ourselves without being dragged down by others constantly.

We've already touched upon what this will mean for your friendship circle, but what about romantic relationships?

Until now, you've probably gone out on dates and had a drink to give you confidence and lighten the mood. This is totally counterintuitive when you think about it – alcohol compromises your thinking, makes it hard for you to make good decisions and increases reckless behaviour. None of that is a good thing when you're out with a potential romantic partner, yet so many people drink anyway.

If that's you, how's it been working out for you? If you're anything like me, booze wrecked any chance of developing a solid relationship. When I've had a few drinks, I go from confident to arrogant, transforming into a brash, loud, stupid version of my true self.

When you mix drinks and dating, one of two things usually happens – you like the other person but ruin your chances because you're not being yourself, or you don't particularly like them, but you take things further anyway because your beer goggles tell you it's a good thing! Your intuition has no chance of figuring out whether there is any actual chemistry because the chemicals in alcohol are falsely binding you together (and sometimes stopping any physical binding because you are suffering from brewer's droop or dry vagina!).

If you're always drinking when dating, you're ruining your chances of meeting the right person. You're not being yourself – and neither are they. While sober dating doesn't make you immune to nightmare dates, it gives you a much better chance of connecting with someone you could fall in love with and helps you avoid making those disastrous decisions that see you waking up the next morning filled with regret.

If someone doesn't like you without a couple of drinks inside you, they're not the one for you. It's that simple.

A word of warning – jumping from relationship to relationship because it makes you feel secure, even if your gut instinct keeps telling you the relationship isn't right, is a form of co-dependency. This is one of the BIGGEST addictions in the world, and to a large extent, we all want to be loved and made to feel secure, so we tolerate it, even though we know deep down it's not who we truly want to be with.

This is your opportunity to become more self-aware of how you feel in relationships, find out who you truly are and find someone who complements that new version (partners should fill you with energy – not detract from it!).

Dating is a complete mind field which comes with layers of stress, so if you need to take time away from it, to figure this sober thing out, then nobody is rushing you. Do what you need to do to stay sober, then jump back into dating when the time is right.

Now, you may already be in a long-term relationship when you decided to go sober. This can bring an entirely different set of challenges, especially if your relationship is founded on alcohol.

Removing alcohol from the equation may mean you discover you have nothing in common with your partner without it. If all you've ever done is drink when you're spending time together, you may not have a clue who your partner really is – and vice versa.

Things are bound to change in your relationship when you go sober. It's inevitable. But it may well improve, and you could find yourself enjoying a closeness you never imagined possible.

Part of this will come down to your partner's relationship with alcohol, and that's something out of your control. They may well decide to join you in your sober efforts. They might see the positive changes you're experiencing and be inspired to follow your lead. Or maybe they don't drink that much, and it's not that big a deal for them not to drink at all.

Going sober together can mean you both get to enjoy the health benefits, more money, much more time, 70% more energy – and the improved sex life that doesn't come with floppy dick and dry vagina ruining your evenings. All things that allow any relationship to blossom and thrive.

But it's also possible it could go in the opposite direction. It could be you've both been using alcohol to avoid dealing with your emotions, and your partnership simply isn't ready to go there. If you're sober and your partner is drinking heavily, it's bound to lead to conflict. If so, you must prepare for some potentially rocky times.

I can't look in a crystal ball and tell you what will happen. No two relationships are the same. You've been with your partner long enough to gauge what their reaction is likely to be to you going sober. It's possible that if you stop drinking and they don't, you'll naturally drift apart, if only for the sake of your sobriety. Just to note - you might start resenting them if they continue drinking, which will deplete your energy levels and make you more susceptible to drinking again. Remember to add your partner to the resentments list if they bring any resentments up for you (it could be multiple things they do and part of why you drink – to avoid discussing it with them).

You might want to suggest to your partner they quit drinking with you so you can enjoy the journey together. Or you might want to prepare yourself for the possibility that your relationship might not last the distance when you choose to put your health first.

Without speaking to them about how you feel, they can't read your mind, so have those difficult conversations because they will ultimately benefit both of you in the long term. Never let anyone else compromise your happiness (even long-term partners).

Whatever happens, know that when you quit alcohol, you discover a confidence in yourself you never knew was there. You discover what makes you happy, and it comes from the inside without needing to rely on anyone else (or the crutch of alcohol). That's a strong foundation for improving an existing relationship or finding new love.

Question for the day – start to think about alcohol and your current and past relationships – What role has alcohol played in your relationships? Has alcohol always been the central part of how you would relax, have fun, commiserate, celebrate and so on with your partner? What would those times look like if you removed alcohol?

This question will get you to consciously look at the pattern of alcohol behaviour in your relationships.

There are no right or wrong answers – just more self-awareness.

Journal Space To Write

Journal Space To Write

Evening Journal

This evening I feel:

What could you have done better today?

Did you feel triggered to drink today? If so, what triggered you to think about drinking?

What did you do well today to maintain your sobriety?

Day 20

Morning Journal

Today I feel:

I am grateful for:

1.

2.

3.

My sobriety today may be challenged by:

1.

2.

3.

How can I stay sober today?

1.

2.

3.

Day 20: The Sober Glow

"You Look Great!" – Every person who sees someone they haven't seen for a while after they got sober.

Puffy eyes. Dry, cracked lips. Greasy skin. Nothing beats the hangover look, right?

If you've been drinking for a long time, you probably don't like what you see when you look in the mirror. Back when I was drinking, I avoided taking selfies because I didn't like how I looked in the photos. I looked – and felt – so much older than a young man in my 20s. Hard partying takes its toll sooner than you'd think.

Most people know that drinking is harmful to the liver, but not so many understand the impact on the rest of the body. Look at before and after pictures of people who've gone sober, and you'll see they all have one thing in common: they have that sober glow! They look healthy, with clear skin and a sparkle in their eyes. Just look at the #transformationtuesday on social media, and there will be a big group of unbearable sober types who love sharing their epic physical transformations (and why not!).

Alcohol negatively impacts the skin in numerous ways. It has a dehydrating effect, making you look bloated and puffy. Poor sleep quality gives you bags under the eyes, while the alcohol can also give you a red, flushed appearance. Sometimes, this can turn into rosacea, which may become a long-term issue or rhinophyma, the posh term for "alcoholic's nose".

Some drinkers get an allergic reaction to alcohol, which brings on hives. As if that wasn't enough, alcohol can also cause sun sensitivity, psoriasis, cellulitis, and even skin cancer.

No wonder your reflection doesn't look great the morning after the night before.

The good news is that there's a simple solution: stop drinking. And if you've been able to stick with it, you should have started seeing the difference already. You may have had people compliment you on how you seem brighter and more radiant. The sober glow gets 'glowier' the more you practice positive feedback loops so make sobriety a lifestyle choice because your body will thank you for it.

Isn't it a great feeling when someone tells you how you look so much younger than you really are? I'll tell you something else too – that feeling never gets old.

Action for the day – Look at the worst photo you have taken in the last six months and use that as your motivation for getting sober. Keep it close, and if you ever feel triggered, use that as a quick motivation to move your actions back towards sobriety.

The sober glow is very real, and while results will differ from person to person, regular exercise, eating more healthily and staying sober are the three most powerful things you can do to keep that sober glow.

Just to note – results don't happen overnight. If you have been drinking/drugging/smoking for a long time, it will take time to reverse that damage. It took me 3 months to see good results and it was a year of being consistent with my sobriety, the gym and being more active generally to see massive changes – just be consistent with it all for best results. Over time, the results will SHOCK you, and you can be super proud of how much you have changed.

Evening Journal

This evening I feel:

What could you have done better today?

Did you feel triggered to drink today? If so, what triggered you to think about drinking?

What did you do well today to maintain your sobriety?

Day 21

Morning Journal

Today I feel:

I am grateful for:

1.

2.

3.

My sobriety today may be challenged by:

1.

2.

3.

How can I stay sober today?

1.

2.

3.

Day 21: The Opportunity Cost Of Alcohol

Sobriety is a lot like pizza. When it's good, it's really good. When it's bad, it's still pretty damn good – Unknown.

The opportunity cost of something is what you lose when you choose one option over another. So when you choose alcohol, you might initially have thought you were choosing a life of fun times and socialising.

But what did you really choose?

First, there's the cost of a drink. Alcohol is *expensive!* A night on the town can easily run into three figures, and what have you got to show for it? Good memories? That's assuming you can remember anything at all through the haze of alcohol and if you didn't make a fool of yourself while you were drunk. Again, it's unlikely you would be here if that lifestyle consistently delivered good times (especially if you are over 30 years old – the hangovers might almost last the entire week!).

It's not just money though. There's also the time spent thinking about when you're going to get your next drink, calling round your friends to organise a night out, going out (or staying in) and spending the evening drinking yourself into oblivion. And what have you got to show for it?

Fuck all.

All that time you wasted drinking could have been spent working towards your dreams. If one of your reasons for drinking is because you're unhappy with your life, getting sober frees you up to do something about it. Make a positive change, and look forward to getting up in the morning.

Opportunity cost also has a compound effect which can be negative and positive.

Imagine going out three times a week, spending all that money, energy and feeling the horrendous negatives of alcohol the next day. All that time has been spent on drinking alcohol. If that's what you do year after year, the opportunity cost of time is quickly stacking up against anything else outside of alcohol.

I wasted half a year of my life talking about, doing and recovering from the aftereffects of alcohol and drugs. HALF A YEAR! And to make it even worse, that was probably half a year for at least 10 years of heavy drinking and drugging. Almost five years lost to the control of alcohol! It's hardly surprising I was very much a passenger in my own life story for all that time.

FIVE YEARS!

Now I don't have hangovers or spend half a week talking about what bars/nightclubs we are going to over the weekend; I have managed to write a book series, run a publishing business, play golf 5 days a week, save money (which is incredible for someone who has been bankrupt), have the freedom to go to the gym at any time in the day, help manage the Sober On A Drunk Planet Community and all those things bring me a tremendous amount of joy.

None of that would have been achievable in my old life – mainly because I was too depressed from using alcohol and drugs to think about anything other than getting through the day alive. The opportunities that sobriety will allow you are endless and fulfilling – the polar opposite of alcohol.

The past has gone, and we have no control over it. So forget about what could have been. Now it's time to focus on what can be, and staying sober for 24 hours at a time will allow you to benefit from the time, energy and money that you once wasted on alcohol to do the things you have always dreamed about.

Being sober will give you so much time, energy and money. Can you really afford to lose any more of that to alcohol?

Question for the day – write down how many hours a week you used to spend talking about, planning, drinking and recovering from alcohol and/or drugs below. When you see how much time you spend a week, you can multiply this by 52 weeks and then work out how many days a year using the example below.

Example: I reckon I spent a minimum of 3 days a week in the control of alcohol/drugs, which is 72 hours (1 day = 24 hours). For example, I went out Friday night, woke up hungover Saturday morning, but then went back out again until I came home at about 8am on Sunday morning (those taxi rides were the worst!). I was then hungover all day Sunday and a zombie for all of Monday (and most of the week by the end of my drinking). This doesn't take into account holidays where we would spend all 7 days under the control of alcohol (especially if you went to an all-inclusive!).

72 hours x 52 weeks = 3744 hours and there are 24 hours in a day so you can then divide 3744 by 24 = 156 days a year (and this is an underestimated amount of time!). That's not far off half a year!

Can you give up half a year of your life to alcohol and expect to be living your dream life?

No.

Hopefully, by this point of the Challenge – you see the point: alcohol/drugs are a BIG waste of time that you could spend on something that is actually fulfilling and makes your soul sing.

Start thinking about what you could do with all that time in sobriety – you are allowed to get excited about a fulfilling life outside of alcohol's control!

Another saying about sobriety is *"sobriety delivers everything that alcohol promises"* – how true it is!

Journal Space To Write

Journal Space To Write

Evening Journal

This evening I feel:

What could you have done better today?

Did you feel triggered to drink today? If so, what triggered you to think about drinking?

What did you do well today to maintain your sobriety?

Day 22

Morning Journal

Today I feel:

I am grateful for:

1.

2.

3.

My sobriety today may be challenged by:

1.

2.

3.

How can I stay sober today?

1.

2.

3.

Day 22: The Compound Effect Of Staying Sober

"You will never change your life until you change something you do daily. The secret of your success is found in your daily routine." Darren Hardy – The Compound Effect.

Building on what we considered yesterday, the benefits of sobriety compound over time.

Let's say you spend three days a week planning your next bender, going out partying and then recovering from a night out. If you're anything like me, three days is an underestimate, but you'll see my point in a moment.

Those three days add up to 156 days a year – that's five months! Five months you could have been doing anything other than getting wasted. You could have learned a new skill, read books, spent time at the gym, and done so many things to improve yourself and your life. Instead, you drank it all away.

But just as drinking's negative effects add up without you even thinking about it, the positive effects of sobriety also add up – and fast.

For a start, you regain all the time you were losing to booze. You start feeling more inspired. You have more energy to do all the things you promised yourself to do, only to fall into a bottle instead. Even if you aren't hitting the gym, when you eliminate alcohol from your system, you start feeling better on every level – physical, emotional and mental – and that feeling only gets stronger.

If you've ever tried Dry January, Dry July or Sober October, you'll know it only takes a few weeks for you to feel more energised and start appreciating all the extra time you have now you're not nursing a hangover. Sadly, many people complete Dry January/Dry July/Sober October...

...and celebrate by hitting the bottle! They go back to their old habits so they don't get to discover that the best is still to come.

Your goal of "just one day" will have a massively transformational effect on your life. When you choose to be sober for 24 hours over and over again for weeks, months, and years, you'll see how much you can do, and those achievements stack up. You will create a life that you don't want to escape from, and staying sober becomes easier because of that.

You'll feel proud of yourself because you'll see there's nothing you can't do when you set your mind to it. You can do 24 hours. Keep going – you have done so well to get to this point, and the benefits will keep coming for days, months and years of staying sober!

Question for the day – think about your daily routines around alcohol. What routines could you change to help you stay sober?

Have a think about what routine you could do that can help put your sobriety first (this journal is a great first step), e.g. swapping late nights for early nights, reading instead of drinking, going for a walk around the same time you would open your first beer, attend an exercise class instead of picking up your nightly wine from the supermarket and generally changing up your old ways.

You have got to this point because whatever you are doing might not work, so it's time to develop new healthy routines to help you stay sober and win this Challenge.

Journal Space To Write

Journal Space To Write

Evening Journal

This evening I feel:

What could you have done better today?

Did you feel triggered to drink today? If so, what triggered you to think about drinking?

What did you do well today to maintain your sobriety?

Day 23

Morning Journal

Today I feel:

I am grateful for:

1.

2.

3.

My sobriety today may be challenged by:

1.

2.

3.

How can I stay sober today?

1.

2.

3.

Day 23: Life Is A DIY Project

No one is coming to save you, there is no such thing as a hero, there is only you deciding that you are worthy – Marine Ashnalikyan.

The biggest lesson that hit me when I got sober was that life is a DIY (Do It Yourself) project. Nobody will save you or come live your life for you. They're all too busy trying to figure it out for themselves.

The reality is that we're all just muddling through, doing our best. Life can be really challenging, and it's no wonder that so many of us fall into a bottle for temporary relief.

Using alcohol as a form of temporary relief is, by definition, only temporary. Ignoring your problems won't make them go away. If anything, it'll make them get bigger. Drowning your emotions only makes them come back harder when you sober up.

You've probably heard of the saying "sweeping your problems under the carpet," and alcohol allows you to forget about how big and potentially unmanageable that carpet has grown!

At some point, you've got to be brave and tackle whatever you're carrying face on (otherwise alcohol will control you forever). You don't have to do it alone. There is a lot of help available. You just have to ask. There are helplines you can call, charities you can contact, support groups you can join, and online groups where you can post anonymously; there is so much help if you just ask.

It all starts with you deciding you're worthy. You deserve better than drinking your life away. While confronting your feelings head-on might feel scary or overwhelming, I promise you that when you finally face them, it's nowhere near as frightening as you thought it could be. And when you do start to process your issues in a healthy way, life gets so much better.

But you have to be the one to fix yourself. Life really is the ultimate DIY project. You are the star of your own movie.

Question for the day – You are the star in your own movie – write a brief synopsis of what that movie looks like without alcohol?

Manifestation used to be one of those words I would cringe at. But then I got sober and achieved more things in the first few years of my sobriety than I had managed in the previous thirty years on this drunk planet. It goes beyond just my story; just look at all the sober communities and sober celebs that become achievers when they get sober. The road isn't easy, but showing yourself you can get sober is the first goal that hopefully ignites a passion for achieving more goals.

Up to now, you have been a slave to the booze culture that keeps you in a negative feedback loop of drink > lose time > lose money > feel depressed > repeat; you now have the chance to break that cycle and write a new and exciting story (that doesn't involve any hangovers!).

Journal Space To Write

Journal Space To Write

Evening Journal

This evening I feel:

What could you have done better today?

Did you feel triggered to drink today? If so, what triggered you to think about drinking?

What did you do well today to maintain your sobriety?

Day 24

Morning Journal

Today I feel:

I am grateful for:

1.

2.

3.

My sobriety today may be challenged by:

1.

2.

3.

How can I stay sober today?

1.

2.

3.

Day 24: Sobriety Is Steroids For Your Career

"Sobriety gives you a new unwavering sense of direction and drive. You will either excel in your current job or have the drive to find a job that you will excel in" – Sean Alexander.

It's sad but true: most people don't enjoy their job. It's called hard work for a reason, right?

Yet most of us spend most of our adulthood working – on average, over 200 days every year. What a tragic waste of life if you're miserable all that time. Then throw in the time spent drinking and hungover, all to help you get through the day. So whatever disposable income you have, you end up drinking, leaving you with nothing to help you get ahead. You feel stuck and turn to drink even more to get you through.

You tell yourself that if you just earned more, it would all be okay, but more money doesn't solve anything. We tend to expand our lifestyles to match our salaries. That's why many high earners are stuck in jobs they hate because they need to pay the mortgage or their kids' school fees. It's what happens when you get into the rat race to keep up with the Joneses.

306

Of course, this can still happen even if you're sober. Not drinking doesn't mean you have your dream job or aren't materialistic. But you've got a heck of a lot more chance of figuring out what you want and getting it when alcohol isn't clouding your brain and making you turn up like a zombie every day.

Living your life somewhere between being drunk and nursing a hangover is hardly a great tactic for trying to climb the career ladder. Many people have wrecked their chances of promotion thanks to drunken nights out. Get the wrong kind of reputation, and you'll find it hard to progress without switching companies – and even then, your reputation may have preceded you.

Many a deal might have been done over a drink, but you'll find that the ones who are quickly scaling the career ladder are the ones who know when to call it quits and don't come to work hungover the following day.

They might not say anything, but people notice the difference between someone who shows up at work on time, showered and neatly presented with a clear mind ready to tackle the day and someone flopping into their chair ten minutes late, breath stinking of stale booze needing three cups of coffee before they can even think about getting stuck into their to-do list (sorry not sorry to people I used to "work" with).

They remember these things when deciding who gets more responsibility or how big their bonus will be this year.

Days that start well tend to finish well. When you don't drink, you don't have to worry about pushing through a hangover; you have many more good days at work than bad.

Those good days add up (the sober compound effect again). The clear head you get from not drinking enables you to perform at your best. You can process information faster and remember the important little details. As you go for longer without a drink, more and more people notice these positive improvements and more opportunities come your way. You become more confident in your ability to deliver, so you speak up more and put yourself in opportunities' way by applying for that promotion or a better job.

This also works if you're self-employed. You might not be answerable to a boss, but your clients and customers will appreciate your products and services more because as you start improving yourself, your business improves right along with you.

Whatever your employment status, your job will only get better when you take alcohol out of the equation. You might even discover – like I did – that you're in the wrong career and find something that speaks to your soul in a way your old job never could.

You spend too long at work to hate what you do. Dream big. You're worth it.

Question of the day – Do you enjoy all seven days of the week? If not, why not?

Think about your energy at work, the people you work with and really think deeply about whether spending time in that environment makes you happy/sad/angry (use the emotions wheel if need be).

Sobriety will give you the time, energy and radical clarity to start a career you truly want and one that aligns with your intentions. When your intentions align with your purpose, and that's what you do each day, it never feels like work (I never believed people when they used to say that to me – but it's true!).

Top tip: Don't just quit your job after reading this. We all need money and a sensible exit plan if we have bills to pay, so think rationally, not emotionally, when it comes to your job (I had my sober awakening and handed my notice the next day – not advisable!).

Moving jobs is a BIG deal, which comes with new stresses as well as new interactions around being 'sober', which may leave you feeling more susceptible to drinking when facing questions from new work colleagues. Make sure you only move jobs when you feel more secure in your sobriety and can take on the extra stress that starting a new job or business entails (and from experience, it's lots of stress!).

Journal Space To Write

Journal Space To Write

Evening Journal

This evening I feel:

What could you have done better today?

Did you feel triggered to drink today? If so, what triggered you to think about drinking?

What did you do well today to maintain your sobriety?

Day 25

Morning Journal

Today I feel:

I am grateful for:

1.

2.

3.

My sobriety today may be challenged by:

1.

2.

3.

How can I stay sober today?

1.

2.

3.

Day 25: Feeling Good, Complacency And Your Ego

I'm very serious about no alcohol, no drugs. Life is too beautiful – Jim Carrey.

If you've stuck with your commitment to stay sober, you've had over three weeks without a drink. Congratulations! If you drank like I used to, I never went more than three days without a drink for over twenty years – so three weeks is EPIC.

But now is the time for me to give you a warning. You see, at the moment, you're probably feeling amazing. And so you should! You've been sober for 25 days. You'll have noticed the improvement in your health. You'll feel better about yourself. You'll be noticing all the positive changes around you.

And this is the time when you're at the greatest risk of going back to the booze. Yes, we spoke about it earlier, and it's my favourite topic in sobriety – the ego.

You see, right now, your ego will be flying high. It'll be loving all the compliments you're getting on how great you look. It'll be thriving on how well you're doing at work. It'll be expanding like nobody's business because things are going so well (or at least better than when you were hungover and unhappy).

Which is right when your ego will try to trip you up. Something will happen, one of your triggers will occur, and you'll hear that little voice in your head that says, "you can have just one drink." Trust me – you really can't!

History has shown you that it's never just one drink. Unlike a Financial Advisor who has to tell you that "past investment performance is not an indicator of future performance", I am telling you, as a counsellor and former drunk, that past drinking performance is the strongest indicator of future drinking performance! Don't let your ego fool you.

You don't want all that hard work, self-awareness and sobriety to be ruined. It's the gift that keeps on giving and requires you to stay sober for 24 hours, which compounds over time along with all the amazing benefits.

By this point, you should hopefully want to move away from that vicious downward spiral that got you to day one of this journal:

Drink > do something stupid > feel lethargic all of the next day > endure a splitting headache > regret > repeat.

When you're aware of all the sneaky little tricks your ego deploys to suck you back into your old ways, you are better equipped to resist it. This is why I put so much emphasis on self-awareness. If you can identify your ego when it rears its ugly head, you can thank it for its concern – and then ignore it. You can turn to one of the strategies you put in place to help you get through when you feel the call of alcohol.

"Assumption is the mother fucker of all fuck ups" (possibly said in a Samuel L Jackson movie, but I can't verify it).

Never assume you will be ok. Never assume you will never be triggered again after doing a 31-day Challenge. Never assume that your last rock bottom was the worst – it can always get worse.

Sobriety takes continued work, especially as we fight this drunken planet's perception of alcohol and the ACTUAL harm it's doing to people every day. Always be mindful that alcohol is everywhere and woven into society's cultural identity – we can't escape it, but we can consciously control our actions around it – this involves not getting complacent about its potential to control us again.

Remember: Just one day. It's all you have to focus on.

Question for the day - Write down five things that will help you tackle complacency around alcohol rearing its ugly head.
For example, you could top up your sobriety book collection to gain a fresh perspective and reminder of how bad alcohol actually is. It will help keep sobriety at the top of your thoughts (Sober On A Drunk Planet has lots of books for you!).

Start going to AA/SMART Recovery meetings. Join a sober meetup, online group and become more involved around sober people, talking about sober things and keeping sobriety an integral part of your life.

Yes, you can also get a tattoo of the Sober On A Drunk Planet logo of a broken bottle if you wish as a reminder ;) The logo symbolises breaking free from alcohol's control, and it's a constant reminder of why I want to stay sober (I also printed it on all my golf balls because I am either playing golf or writing!).

Here it is in case you want to show the tattoo artist what to do:

Disclaimer — It's your choice if you get a tattoo of the broken bottle or any tattoo, so only get it if you want it!

If you get a tattoo done, share a photo of it in the Sober On A Drunk Planet Community!

Journal Space To Write

Journal Space To Write

Evening Journal

This evening I feel:

What could you have done better today?

Did you feel triggered to drink today? If so, what triggered you to think about drinking?

What did you do well today to maintain your sobriety?

Day 26

Morning Journal

Today I feel:

I am grateful for:

1.

2.

3.

My sobriety today may be challenged by:

1.

2.

3.

How can I stay sober today?

1.

2.

3.

Day 26: Understanding And Managing Cross Addiction

She goes from one addiction to another. All are ways for her not to feel her feelings – Ellen Burstyn.

Addiction is a disease, and it's one that we don't fully understand. When it has you in its clutches, it doesn't want to let you go.

This is why, when we conquer one addiction, it's common to replace it with something else, whether that be food, sex, gambling, online shopping, social media, or anything else that helps us avoid whatever we were using alcohol to hide from.

We can justify it as "not being as bad" as drinking and drugging. While that might be true regarding the chaos attached to it, it still patches over that wound we spoke about earlier in this Challenge and will always bubble on the surface if left untreated.

I've become self-aware through working the 3 sober steps that sobriety has seen me turn to food, probably my first addictive substance I used as a child to cover up feelings of sadness as a result of being bullied. It's the most common cross addiction because it's so readily available and accepted. You might have even noticed your own intake of sweets go sky-high since quitting booze (it's the most asked question in the community – how can I stop eating so many sweets!).

It's not uncommon to share stories about how we devoured a whole family-share bag of chocolate, with no family present, and regretted it immediately the next day (a familiar cycle you see with alcohol!). I've used the same three steps mentioned in '3 Sober Steps', to overcome my cross addiction to food by learning about my biology and what foods work well with it. I have then taken action to change the way I cook and to limit the takeaways, and this has fed my intuition on what is healthier for me as a result. No more mindless eating, and my weight has remained consistent for the longest time since I was born! The 3 sober steps work for any addictive substance, not just alcohol/drugs.

Work addiction has crept in because I have suffered from burnout a few times since getting sober – who would have thought that launching eight books across thirty countries in just over a year would have led to burnout?!

Thirdly, the most time-consuming cross-addiction is my phone and social media. Through the three-step process, I have limited social media to only managing the Sober On A Drunk Planet Community – because without doing that, I have wasted hours upon hours of mindlessly scrolling. I have addictive genetics, and anything designed to keep you scrolling is dangerous for me (and likely for you as well).

Sure, all these additional cross-addictions might not be as chaotic as getting drunk every night, but it's still a form of self-destructive behaviour that's going to take its toll on you and fulfilling your dreams. You decided to go sober because you wanted a better life. That's only going to happen when you dig deep into the reasons why you turned to alcohol in the first place.

The purpose of this whole process is to heal whatever is causing that underlying itch that has you turning to alcohol, food, drugs, whatever. It doesn't matter whether you're trying to bury trauma or you've got something else to deal with. It's time to stop running and face up to it so you can bury it once and for all.

The end game is to move forward without relying on a crutch – no mindless internet shopping, no mindless scrolling through social media for hours, and no overeating Chinese takeaway again!

If you thought you could get through this process without facing up to the things you've been hiding from, think again. Yes, it's hard. Yes, it'll feel uncomfortable. This is why you'll probably want to get help. In my case, I went to rehab and have used forms of therapy ever since – they are the greatest acts of self-care I have done for myself.

But you need to understand the underlying causes of your drinking. You need to heal. Otherwise, you'll find you're simply swapping one addiction for another, and nobody wants that.

Question for the day – What other substances do you mindlessly use? Do you eat a packet of cookies without even thinking about it? Why do you scroll for hours on social media? Have you been working longer hours to avoid uncomfortable emotions at home? Do you REALLY need that gadget that you saw on a TikTok video?

When you do the work, like finding out social media companies hire psychology specialists to get users hooked (corporate drug dealers?!), it starts to give you the power to make better-informed choices that align with your intentions and goals.

Journal Space To Write

Journal Space To Write

Evening Journal

This evening I feel:

What could you have done better today?

Did you feel triggered to drink today? If so, what triggered you to think about drinking?

What did you do well today to maintain your sobriety?

Day 27

Morning Journal

Today I feel:

I am grateful for:

1.

2.

3.

My sobriety today may be challenged by:

1.

2.

3.

How can I stay sober today?

1.

2.

3.

Day 27: Becoming Emotionally Mature

Maturity is achieved when a person postpones immediate pleasures for long-term values – Joshua L. Liebman.

This journal has been designed to help you understand your emotions and how they can change throughout the day. This self-awareness will help you identify your triggers so you can put strategies in place to find better ways of coping with them.

Managing your emotions and responding to them logically is a key skill essential to long-term sobriety. The work that you are doing will see you become more emotionally mature so that over time you'll find it easier and easier to handle your triggers.

But how do you know when you're becoming emotionally mature?

It's a gradual process, and the signs can be subtle, so you might not be aware of all the progress you've made. But don't be fooled into thinking you haven't progressed just because it isn't obvious to you. If you've been doing the work outlined in this journal, you *will* have matured!

Here are some indications that you're emotionally maturing:

- You can see that some people are caught up in negative patterns of behaviour and understand you don't have to join them in their self-destructive habits. This might mean you say no when they ask you out, and that's okay.

- You accept that you are only responsible for how you respond to others and have no control over what they do. You practice regulating your emotions and take full ownership of your decisions. So when your friends pressure you to join them for "just one drink", you say no instead of undoing all your hard work.

- You realise that people are free to make their own choices. You appreciate that it's not up to you to try to change others or force them to share your opinions.
  When you get sober, you want nothing more than to get all your friends to see for themselves how great it is. It won't take long before you'll see you can't force anyone to change. They've got to want to do it themselves.

- You can handle differences of opinion. You understand that someone can think completely differently to you, and that's okay.
- You allow yourself the time and space to respond so you can consider your options to make an informed decision instead of blindly reacting.
- You set up healthy emotional boundaries and enforce them without feeling guilty or worrying about hurting others' feelings. You ditch the people-pleasing and prioritise your sobriety.
- You can let go of things that would have seen you reaching for a drink in the past.

If you're observing some of these points in your daily sobriety, you're becoming more emotionally mature. Keep going!

Question for the day - What have you learned about your emotions since taking on this Challenge?

It's important to remember with all these questions that there are no right or wrong answers, just more self-awareness.

Journal Space To Write

Journal Space To Write

Evening Journal

This evening I feel:

What could you have done better today?

Did you feel triggered to drink today? If so, what triggered you to think about drinking?

What did you do well today to maintain your sobriety?

Day 28

Morning Journal

Today I feel:

I am grateful for:

1.

2.

3.

My sobriety today may be challenged by:

1.

2.

3.

How can I stay sober today?

1.

2.

3.

Day 28: The Sunday Scaries Disappear And Sunday Funday Actually Becomes FUN

*Smonday (n.): That moment when Sunday stops feeling like a Sunday and the anxiety of Monday kicks in –
Unknown.*

Back when I was working in finance, Sunday nights were almost as bad as Monday mornings. I'd start filling up with a sense of existential dread, the thought of the week ahead making me almost overwhelmingly anxious on top of the fact I was hungover to high heaven and just finished gurning from another weekend off my head.

The "Sunday Scaries" describe how you feel when you've had yet another long week at work, so you binge-drink from Friday night to Sunday morning, leaving you lying in bed all Sunday, questioning everything about your life. You go over all the things you regret and wonder whether this is as good as you get. You spend the whole of Sunday filled with angst, asking yourself why you can't seem to catch a break – all the while fighting off your latest hangover and dreading the fact you have work tomorrow.

And sometimes, if it was a really BIG weekend, I would go to the pub all day and night on Sunday and call it "Sunday Funday".

Nothing about Monday (or the rest of the week) was fun because of it. Sunday Funday was just another form of self-harm!

Looking back, it's clear to see that because I hated my life so much, I was stuck in a negative feedback loop where I needed alcohol to cope, but the drink would make things worse. Sundays should have been a day of rest, recuperation and actual FUN, but instead, they were overshadowed by thoughts of what was to come. Ironically, things might not have been so bad if I hadn't had to deal with all the side effects of alcohol, but at the time, it was the only way I knew to get me through the week.

Getting sober enabled me to discover what made my soul light up. The natural confidence I developed as a consequence of getting sober was life-changing for me, and it will be for you.

You *can* enjoy every day equally! You don't have to dread Mondays. Every day offers a brand-new opportunity to do something extraordinary.

That doesn't mean you won't ever have a bad day again. Life comes with its inevitable ups and downs. But when you're sober, you can develop positive coping strategies that help you weather any storm. You'll be able to learn from all your experiences, good and bad, and use them to help you grow and develop.

So what do you want? Another case of the Sunday Scaries or a sober lifestyle where every day can be just as fulfilling as the last? The choice is yours.

Question for the day – Think about how your mood changes from Monday to Sunday. How does that mood coincide with your alcohol use?

When I was drinking/drugging, my mood went something like this – Monday (just make it to Tuesday alive), Tuesday (I started drinking/drugging again because I felt less dead than I did on Monday), Wednesday To Friday (tired, high, hungover, depressed and just trying to make it through each day without getting sacked) and Saturday and Sunday (numb to the world because I was drunk and high for all of it). Not much of a life!

The difference between sobriety and being able to forge your own future is that I have no perception of time, and every day has the potential to be as full of opportunity as the day before. That is a complete mindset change from having to work Monday to Friday and watching the clock countdown to 5pm to then getting shit-faced in the pub after work, to forget about the week from hell I just had.

Every day might have felt like "hump day" by the end of your drinking, but sobriety allows you to enjoy Monday – Sunday with excitement and optimism.

Journal Space To Write

Journal Space To Write

Evening Journal

This evening I feel:

What could you have done better today?

Did you feel triggered to drink today? If so, what triggered you to think about drinking?

What did you do well today to maintain your sobriety?

Day 29

Morning Journal

Today I feel:

I am grateful for:

1.

2.

3.

My sobriety today may be challenged by:

1.

2.

3.

How can I stay sober today?

1.

2.

3.

Day 29: Sober NOT Boring!

Being hungover, depressed and broke is boring – A former drunk.

We live on a drunk planet. Alcohol has wound its way into every aspect of our lives. There's always a reason to drink. Drink to celebrate. Drink to commiserate. Drink to feel better. Drink to forget about it.

And if you *don't* drink, you've got to cope with the accusations of being boring, a killjoy, a buzzkill. People love to criticise you when you choose not to drink. It's becoming more socially acceptable now, but even so. It's like there's something suspicious about someone who doesn't drink, or people subconsciously know that their own drinking is a problem, but rather than confront their issues, they take it out on you.

The truth is nothing is boring about being sober. Quite the opposite – it's a lot more fun than being depressed, hungover, skint and a prisoner to alcohol!

The common misperception is that you have to "give up" things when you get sober. But the actual truth is that you are giving up the negative impacts of alcohol (and there are lots from the physical, mental, financial, spiritual and emotional challenges it presents), and we stand to benefit from more time, energy and money (plus everything else stated in "*Giving Up Alcohol*").

Sobriety gives you the opportunity to do anything and everything with your life. Everything is better when your mind is clear and fresh.

Once you discover what you truly love to do and have the confidence to pursue it, there's no holding you back. There's a whole world out there waiting for you to discover it. Go and embrace it!

Question of the day – What would your ideal life look like?

Write down what it would be like, maybe brainstorm keywords and fill it with things that fill your soul with joy. Start to build a picture of why you want to stay sober, why you want more time, energy and money and how that can start helping you create the most incredible future. It's time to start dreaming big – if you can see it, you can achieve it – sobriety allows you the clarity and creativity to do whatever you want!

Journal Space To Write

Journal Space To Write

Evening Journal

This evening I feel:

What could you have done better today?

Did you feel triggered to drink today? If so, what triggered you to think about drinking?

What did you do well today to maintain your sobriety?

Day 30

Morning Journal

Today I feel:

I am grateful for:

1.

2.

3.

My sobriety today may be challenged by:

1.

2.

3.

How can I stay sober today?

1.

2.

3.

Day 30: You are STRONG – the power of positive affirmations.

The self-fulfilling prophecy is real – what you tell yourself, you become. Start being epic to yourself – Sean Alexander.

When I was in active addiction, my inner voice went something like this (about a hundred times a day): "you are worthless, you are not loved, and you are a joke".

Imagine if someone sat you down each day and repeated that sentence over a hundred times every morning to your face before you went to work – it's hardly motivating!

The truth is, you become what you tell yourself you are. Having experienced severe addiction, where I constantly told myself I was useless and a joke – I quickly became hopeless, bankrupt, addicted to all things and extremely broken.

But then I got sober, and the first thing we were told to practice in rehab was to say one positive affirmation each day in front of the mirror – cringe! It felt like sticking needles into my eyes every day because I hated the person

I saw in the mirror, but from a psychological perspective – it cured my destructive inner narrative.

It was very much "face it until you make it" at that stage, so it's important to emphasise that even if you don't believe in yourself now, just trust the process and keep going.

Now, I wake up and have total belief in myself and my abilities. While it sounds too easy, positive affirmations were the BIGGEST part of changing that inner narrative from destructive to becoming someone I admire.

And remember, your thoughts dictate what emotions you feel, and in turn, they dictate what actions you take. So, if you feed yourself negative words, your actions will be negative. Repeat that for a long enough time, and you will find yourself in a dark place (like I did). The flipside is telling yourself positive words, e.g. you can (instead of you can't), you are worthy (instead of worthless), you are capable (instead of you are useless), and you are strong (instead of you are weak).

Question for the day - Think about how your reality is created with your thoughts dictating your emotions, which dictate your actions.

What inner narrative is feeding your thoughts? What are you telling yourself each day? What is the inner voice saying when you are criticised? Praised? Have been made fun of? Get let down by a friend? Get dumped by your partner?

What voice is feeding that initial part of your reality – your thoughts. That has one of the most significant impacts on your life, and it's something you need to practice and become self-aware of if you want to be sober long-term and get ahead in life.

If you are negative about who you are and what you do, your thoughts, emotions, and actions will follow that. You are then creating that reality around how you talk to yourself, a.k.a. the self-fulfilling prophecy.

And yes, having been on both sides of the coin, it really is that simple – start doing positive affirmations each day and give yourself some compassion – life is hard, so don't make it harder by beating yourself up. You should be your number-one cheerleader.

Top Tip: Start doing positive affirmations each morning when you get up and do them in front of the mirror. Tell yourself you are strong, you are loved, you are enough, you can stay sober, and you can be the best version of yourself. You have nothing to lose – just remember to keep eye contact with the mirror (yes, I know, it's cringy as fuck to make eye contact with yourself and be positive, but it works!)

Journal Space To Write

Journal Space To Write

Evening Journal

This evening I feel:

What could you have done better today?

Did you feel triggered to drink today? If so, what triggered you to think about drinking?

What did you do well today to maintain your sobriety?

The Final Day

Day 31

Morning Journal

Today I feel:

I am grateful for:

1.

2.

3.

My sobriety today may be challenged by:

1.

2.

3.

How can I stay sober today?

1.

2.

3.

Day 31: Congratulations On Becoming Sober On A Drunk Planet!

You didn't come this far only to come this far – Unknown.

You've done it! 31 days of sobriety is a HUGE achievement - keep it up!

This Challenge was never designed to just be 31 days of sobriety; it's designed to motivate you to want better for yourself and to see that's only possible by staying sober and continuing to do the work.

If you can do a month, you can do two months. If you can do two, you can do six months. If you can do six months, you can do a year and so on. But the same principle applies – keep your goal to being sober for 24 hours. Over time, you will find it will take up less of your energy, being mindful not to get complacent on a planet obsessed with it all, and you can start moving into more exciting goals to help you create that life you will never want to escape from.

But for now, I want you to do something to celebrate yourself. Give yourself a big pat on the back for coming so far. Or even better, share about it in the Sober On A Drunk Planet Community and get lots of praise (we have all been in the same position as you and understand how amazing an achievement it is!).

It's important to celebrate every little win in sobriety. Affirming positive actions with positive rewards will help reinforce those new neural pathways we're developing, making it easier to maintain your sobriety. Just imagine a new puppy; how do they know they are doing the right thing? They get rewarded for the right behaviour, and the more they do it, the more it happens on autopilot – sobriety and rewards are the same.

So what are you going to do to celebrate? It goes without saying that you won't want to go out and get drunk! But think about all the money you've saved by not drinking this month. You could use that money to go out for a nice meal, see a Theatre show, go on a yoga retreat or maybe even book a city break somewhere. You could even invest in your own health and well-being and sign up for counselling for your mental health and a personal trainer for your physical health (these two are VERY powerful together).

Remember, the compound effect of staying sober keeps building even more amazing benefits, so you have just scratched the service. (I went from bankruptcy to writing and running my own publishing business. I recently started the journey following my childhood dream of playing on the professional golf circuit – all thanks to sobriety and that compound effect!).

There are so many things you can do that don't have to involve drinking. And the great thing is that you'll go out, have fun – and be able to remember all the cool things you got up to!

I'm so proud of you for coming this far. This is just the start. There's a world of opportunities waiting for you now alcohol isn't holding you back.

Top Tip: Keep going with the sobriety. You deserve all the good things in life, and you can have them!

You should close out the Challenge by completing the final reflections, which include the finance tracker on the next page. This will help you become even more self-aware and open your eyes to what you have achieved so far (and can achieve in the future!).

Thank you for being part of this Challenge and we hope sobriety delivers everything for you that alcohol could only promise.

Final Reflections

Throughout this challenge, I've emphasised the importance of self-awareness when getting and staying sober. Now that you've completed 31 days sober, it's worth reflecting on your experiences. This will help you see how far you've come and help motivate you to keep going.

Use the prompts below to consider everything you've learned over the past month. Again, this is not about being right or wrong; it's about developing your own self-awareness.

- What is your main takeaway from these 31 days?

- What are you most proud of?

- What have you learned about yourself over the past 31 days?

- What do you understand about your triggers now that you didn't know before?

- What changes have you noticed over the last 31 days in each of these areas?
  - Mentally

  - Physically

  - Spiritually

- Emotionally

- Financially

- Relationships

What can you do to support your sobriety moving forward?

Finance Tracker – The (Shock) Calculation

Use the amount you calculated at the beginning of this journal and multiply it by 4 – this gives you an amount you would spend in a month. Then, use that monthly total to complete the table below:

How much did I save this month? (Example: Week amount x 4 = £/$300)	
How much would I save in six months? (Multiply the amount you saved this month by 6) (Example: £/$300 x 6 = £/$1800)	
How much would I save in a year? (Multiply the amount you saved this month by 12) (Example: £/$300 x 12 = £/$3,600)	

If you had saved that money in an account paying 5% interest, how much money would you have now? (Multiply the amount you saved in a year by 1.025.) (Example: £/$3,600 x 1.025 = £/$3,690)	
And how much money would you have saved in 5 years? (Take the amount you saved in a year, multiply it by 5, and multiply it again by 1.136 to give you the total you would save in five years with interest applied). (Example: £/$3,600 x 5 = £/$18,000 x 1.136 = £/$20,448)	
And how much money would you have saved in 10 years? (Take the amount you saved in a year, multiply it by 10, and multiply it again by 1.297 to give you the total you would save in ten years' time with interest applied). (Example: £/$3,600 x 10 = £/$36,000 x 1.297 = £/$46,692)	

What are you going to do with all that money?

You could invest it in furthering your education, health and fitness, starting a business or investing in your existing one, treating your family, buying your first property, or whatever appeals to you the most.

When you get sober and invest (not waste) money on your health and well-being, you see it repays 10x over when compared to drinking alcohol. The two couldn't be further apart in terms of self-care and growth! Self-care should become a priority, and you can start going to spa weekends to ACTUALLY relax and rejuvenate rather than needing another two weeks off work from a weekend of partying in Ibiza (true story).

I'm going to invest my money on:

Leave A Review

If you have enjoyed this challenge, I would be grateful if you could spare 60 seconds to leave a short review on Amazon, even if it's just a few sentences, using the QR codes below:

UNITED STATES

SCAN ME

UNITED KINGDOM

SCAN ME

CANADA

SCAN ME

AUSTRALIA

SCAN ME

Thank you!

Must Read Books

If you want to understand more about the tools to stop drinking and take a deeper dive around the '3 Sober Steps' mentioned, order '**3 Sober Steps**' today by using the QR code below:

Or visit www.soberonadrunkplanet.com/books

If you want to re-affirm why you are doing the sober thing and need a reminder about the benefits of long-term sobriety and what your future could look like without alcohol - Check out the International Bestseller – '**Giving Up Alcohol**' - using the QR code below:

Or visit www.soberonadrunkplanet.com/books

A New Author

If you have enjoyed the Sober On A Drunk Planet Series – we are sure you will love Sienna Green with her Aussie charm and witty outlook on Sobriety.

Start with her groundbreaking first book – Why Don't You Drink Alcohol? 101 Reasons You Should Stop Drinking.

You can order a copy using the QR code below:

Or visit www.soberonadrunkplanet.com/books/

A Personal Note

I just want to personally congratulate you on completing your first 31 days of sobriety. Not everyone has the courage to do what you've just done. You should feel proud of yourself for coming this far.

Remember: you only need to stay sober for 24 hours, and you've already proven you can do it. So, all you need to do now is keep it up.

You've got this. I believe in you, and we have a supportive community who can help you continue your sobriety by scanning the QR code below:

Or visit www.soberonadrunkplanet.com/community

You will hopefully have started to see for yourself why nobody has ever regretted getting sober.

Keep going,

Sean Alexander

P.S. - If you were wondering about the dedication at the front of the book, Patrick was my therapist when I was in rehab. If in doubt, get a therapist – they can really help you turn your life around!

Appendix

a) Emotions Wheel – Use the wheel to identify the emotions you are feeling today.

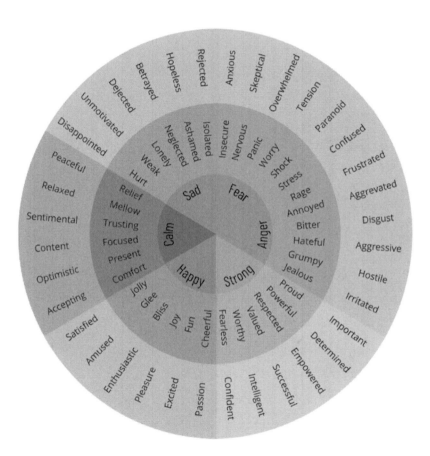

b) Gratitude List – It might be your first time making a gratitude list, so here are some examples to get you going (try to think of new ones each day and think about what you are really grateful for – not material things!)

Today I am grateful for.........

- Being present enough to understand I need assistance in staying sober and wanting to change my life for the better.
- Taking time to understand alcohol's control over my life and wanting to make positive changes.
- Supportive friends who have helped me get to this point with my sobriety.
- My family and helping me through the tough times
- Waking up hangover free away from the chaos and destruction that alcohol had over me (this makes it on my list every day!).
- Living amongst the birds and the bees and enjoying nature for everything it offers.
- The Sober On A Drunk Planet community and the extra support they offer in my sobriety journey (yes, we are shameless in our promotion techniques, but the group is epic!).
- The food that I have on my table every night and understanding that not everyone has this privilege.

- The money in my bank that allows me to go to therapy sessions and work on myself.
- The support of AA/SMART recovery in my journey
- Doing this sobriety journal so I can better myself from the grip of alcohol (and/or drugs).
- Understanding that there is more to life than feeling hungover and depressed and taking the time to want to better myself.
- To give myself the compassion I needed to start this sobriety journey and understand that I needed help.
- That I can enjoy playing (enter sport/hobby) with a clear mind, no hangover and new energy from my sobriety.

c) My sobriety today may be challenged by:
   a. After work drinks celebrating a client win.
   b. A wedding that I have been invited to today.
   c. It's Friday night (any day can be a trigger!), and I have that "Friday Night Feeling" that always results in me getting drunk.
   d. People I work with on a certain project make my job very stressful and I know they can trigger me (add it to your triggers list as well!).
   e. A funeral I need to attend.
   f. My friend has split with her other half; they are my usual drinking buddies.

g. Seeing my family and they will expect me to drink at our gatherings (it is what we have always done together).

h. Planning a holiday with a friend and we have always gone on boozy holidays together and would celebrate booking a holiday with drinks.

i. Playing sport with my team, and they always get drunk afterwards to celebrate a win, loss or draw! This can apply to any sport or hobby.

j. Going to watch my team play, and we would usually meet for drinks beforehand, during and after the match.

k. Going to a stag do/bachelor/hen/bachelorette party that everyone will expect me to drink.

l. Driving past my usual pub/bar that might trigger me to stop and have a drink (again, write this is your trigger list as well).

m. It's thirsty Thursday (yes, we used to call it this), and we always get shit-faced because having a hangover at work on a Friday is better than having it on a Saturday (albeit, it happened Saturday and Sunday anyway)

Be conscious of what challenges each day presents. Don't worry about future challenges past the next 24 hours, as you want to focus all your energy on staying sober for 24 hours.

d) How can I stay sober today (answering the examples from c)):

    a. Make my excuses to the work team about after-work drinks and go to the gym instead.

    b. Politely decline the invite for the wedding while I do this 31-day sobriety challenge – I have to remember that I am doing this for my own happiness, and they should understand (if they ask at all). (Alternatively, if you have to go to it, plan ahead to what alcohol-free options there are, enjoy the wedding, do the dinner and then leave to your hotel room when you start to feel like your sobriety might be compromised)

    c. In order to challenge the Friday night itch, I am going straight to the gym after work and will use exercise to change the way I feel and tire me out. I can then treat myself to a takeaway and a film and enjoy the rest of the weekend.

    d. Try to understand why the emotion of anger comes up for me and see what that means for me (and not to put the blame onto them). Try to keep my space from them while accepting I have to look at our relationship differently now because I don't want my anger towards them to cause me more harm by drinking tonight.

e. Attend the funeral by car, speak to a few people after and then leave if I feel uncomfortable. I might have an alcohol-free option to stop people asking me but equally, I can just have a water and say I am driving.

f. Tell my friend that I can support them but it has to be over a coffee in a coffee shop otherwise we can have a call to discuss it.

g. Say to my family I can't make the gathering or tell them that I have plans later in the evening and can only drive round for a short time so won't be able to drink.

h. Make no plans for a holiday at this stage and just put a clear boundary in place – I am going sober for the moment and not sure what that holiday would look like at the moment. Or just book a sober holiday together (and see how amazing it feels to go away and ACTUALLY relax!).

i. To avoid the after-match drinks, I will drive and say whatever I need to in order to protect my inner peace and sobriety. I could have a few alcohol-free options, but I feel like they might trigger me (add to your list if you need to) to drink actual alcohol at this stage.

j. Drive to the match as your reason to not drink or be questioned about it. Alternatively, you can drink alcohol-free options if they are available.

Or just avoid these meetings until you feel comfortable.

k. Just don't go! Probably the worst thing you could put yourself through when trying to stay sober. Wait until you are 100% confident in your sobriety – the chances are nobody will miss you after they are ten drinks in and handcuffed naked to a street light.

l. Drive a different route away from places that might trigger you. I will take a different route home after work that avoids the bars/pubs that I normally drink at.

m. To avoid Thirsy Thursdays for the short term (hoping they will stop inviting me at some point), I will start training with a personal trainer every Thursday so we can start working towards those physical goals, and I can do some actual work on a Friday for once!

Triggers list continued.......

People	Places	Things

Resentments table continued.......

Who/what do I resent?	What caused my resentment?	What emotion does this make me feel?	What do I achieve by letting this resentment go?
Wendy	*Receiving a higher bonus than me*	*Fearful that I am not good enough*	*Losing energy to something I can't control and to look at my own performance to see where I can improve*

Made in the USA
Monee, IL
18 March 2024

55229023R00221